THERAPY THROUGH
MOVEMENT

Tring desorder
16 f

CONTENTS

CHAPTER 4
THE THERAPEUTIC VALUE OF
MOVEMENT AND DANCE
By Chloe Gardner and Audrey Wethered / 141

CHAPTER 5
DRAMATHERAPY
By Sue Jennings / 189

PREFACE

"Psychomotricity is the experience of the body in action, as it is dynamically structured and integrated in attitudes and gestures while relating to others and the world."
MONIQUE VIDAL

This book has evolved from an increasing awareness on my part that no one therapeutic approach is the answer to any particular disability. Contact with American scientific theories and then the contrasting European views has made me critical of the claims for supremacy of any one particular method or programme.

As an occupational therapist, I am trained to evaluate and modify functional disabilities. The core of my media has always been the moving human body. My dual training in physical medicine and psychiatry has always made me uneasy with a purely physical approach to disablement. Yet experience in recent years has shown me that patients can make considerable psychological progress through purely physical methods. My own special interest in the child with minimal movement disorders and associated learning difficulties began with neuroscience but has developed a far more psychological approach. The opportunity to attend the Psychomotricity Congress in Florence in 1982 brought a widening of my scientific views and a realisation of other possibilities. There followed for me a short investigation of the foundations of psychomotricity. It can best be described as a tree whose roots draw from psychiatry, neurology, education and the creative arts. Through the trunk, these became intermingled and finally extend as therapeutic branches. These branches are in psychiatry, education and physical medicine, but draw from the roots for their resource. The leaves of the tree are the varied methods developed by practitioners and none have grown in isolation of any other. This visual image is part of the use of fantasy that is one aspect of psychomotricity. Another is the role of influence of the therapist and his interaction with the patient. Without fantasy, there could be no 'moon walk'; without interpersonal communication any therapeutic programme becomes a mechanical process.

I have therefore tried to bring together well established and eminent practitioners of some of the recognised therapies, trying to cover the full range from neurophysical to creative. It is hoped that the several areas of overlap and the confidence of the therapists will demonstrate the psychomotricity philosophy. A theme was necessary and what could be more appropriate than the body and its movement. The authors all share with me recognition of the value of their art but also its limitations. The chapters presented cannot cover all the possible therapies using movement as their medium. Neither can the contributors justify much of their work by validated research. If we accept the patient/therapist interaction as the most potent of our 'magic spells' it is extremely difficult to scientifically research our medium effectively. The variables are enormous. The patients described in the following case histories are presented as examples of the practitioner's art. The progress they have made could easily be ascribed to any number of external factors and interventions, or even changes in the patient's social background. They are presented in good faith as examples of the therapy described.

Suzanne Naville, psychomotor therapist from Zurich, Switzerland, has stated "Methodology inhibits the versatility of the therapist, but method is essential to practice". So each of us must create his own structures in presentation of his skill. Although this book is not intended as a Do-It-Yourself manual, it sets out to show the manner in which others have developed their own chosen medium. It is my hope that the reader will find these presentations interesting, that they will be stimulated to discuss the overlap of these professions and the theories and ideologies that support them. Above all, I hope there will be a greater understanding and dialogue between the various disciplines, so it will no longer be the diagnosis that will decide the prescribed therapy but the individuality, inclinations and needs of the patient for whom it is prescribed.

Lorraine A Burr, DipCOT, SROT

CONTRIBUTORS

Priscilla Barclay:
Dalcroze Eurhythmics; Licentiate, DipCOT, MT

Sylvie Barwick:
Diplome d'Etudes Universitaires; Generales de Psychologie.

Lorraine A Burr:
DipCOT, SROT; Head Occupational Therapist (Paediatrics); Harrow District Health Authority, Harrow, Middx.

Chloe Gardner:
DipCOT, SROT; Member of the Laban Guild.

Sue Gretton:
DipCOT, SROT; Senior Occupational Therapist, Paediatrics. Primary Care, Brent District Health Authority.

Sue Jennings:
FRAI, RDTh, LRAM, LGSM, MWMIP; Dramatherapist and Social Anthropologist; Senior Lecturer and course leader of post-graduate Diploma in Dramatherapy at Hertfordshire College of Art and Design, St. Albans, Herts.

Audrey Wethered:
LRAM; Member of the Laban Guild.

Priscilla Barclay

Priscilla Barclay studied Music at the Ecole Normale de Musique in Paris and then gained the Licentiate from the School of Dalcroze Eurhythmics in London. She graduated from the Dorset House School of Occupational Therapy in 1945 and became Occupational Therapist in charge at Cassel Hospital for Functional Nervous Disorders. She left Cassel to explore the use of Music Therapy techniques in the USA.

She was appointed Senior Music Therapist to St. Lawrence Hospital, Caterham in 1956 where she developed the Music Therapy Department. Since her retirement in 1977 Miss Barclay has been an active member of the British Society of Music Therapists. She also lectures and teaches nationwide. Amongst her special interests is the use of Dalcroze Eurhythmics as a music therapy technique with mentally handicapped, autistic and disturbed children and adults.

Sylvie Barwick

Sylvie Barwick is a qualified Pscyhomotor Therapist from France. She graduated in Psychology at the Bordeaux Université de Sciences Humaines; she then studied at the Institute Superieur de Reeducation Psychomotrice in Bordeaux (Soubirhan School) and worked for a year as a Psychomotor Therapist in a Special School (Institute Medico-Educatif).

In 1979 she married her husband, an Englishman, and came to live in England. She is at present working at the Rudolph Steiner School, St. Christopher's, in Bristol.

Lorraine A Burr

Lorraine Burr studied at the London School of Occupational Therapy where she achieved the Dual Diploma of the Association of Occupational Therapists in 1956.

Her career has involved the fields of Psychiatry, Physical Medicine, Domiciliary Visiting and Paediatrics. She joined Northwick Park Hospital in 1971. As part of the development of the service to the Harrow District, she has explored differing European approaches to the treatment of childhood disorders. Concentrating on the field of learning disabilities, she has organised visits to Britain of European specialists. She has also lectured extensively on treatment approaches for the child with minimal movement disorders both in Britain and overseas.

Chloe Gardner

Chloe Gardner graduated in 1944 from the London School of Occupational Therapy. She commenced work in Springfields Hospital, London, in 1945. Having previously trained as a skater, she initially explored Dance based on the concepts of Effort and Space at the Joos Leeder Summer School in 1939. Later, she studied under Rudolph Laban, Lisa Ullman, Warren Lamb and others.

She moved to Friern Hospital, London, in 1950. There, as Deputy Head Occupational Therapist, she continued to relate her knowledge of Laban Movement to the teaching of skills as well as dance and drama.

Although officially retired, Miss. Gardner continues to practise professionally. She is at present studying the use of Laban Movement in the treatment of Hemiplegias. She lectures on the use of Laban Movement as a therapeutic technique.

Sue Gretton

Sue Gretton trained at the Dorset House School of Occupational Therapy. She qualified in 1969 and began training in Paediatrics at the Park Hospital for Children, Oxford, which is the National Centre for Epilepsy.

In 1973, she joined the Spastic Children's Association School in Singapore where she established an Occupational Therapy Department. Whilst abroad, in conjunction with a Physiotherapist, she organised a teaching scheme for university students for working with the profoundly retarded and sensorily deprived child.

As Specialist Occupational Therapist at Guy's Hospital, Newcomen Centre, Mrs. Gretton developed Community Treatments Programmes for handicapped children, including those with motor and learning disabilities. She has since worked at the Central Middlesex Hospital, London, with patients with motor neurone lesions of the brain.

At present, she is Paediatric Community Occupational Therapist (Primary Care) for Brent Area Health Authority.

Sue Jennings

Dramatherapist and Social Anthropologist, Sue Jennings trained as a dancer and actress and performed professionally in the theatre before teaching and then innovating the application of Drama as therapy. She was a founder member of the British Association for Dramatherapy, and held the first Research Fellowship in Dramatherapy at St. John's College, York.

She is a Senior Lecturer and Course Leader in Drama-therapy and Social Anthropology at Hertfordshire College of Art and Design, St. Albans. She also teaches extensively in Europe. Currently, she is completing a doctoral thesis entitled "Drama Ritual and Healing".

Audrey Wethered

Audrey Wethered originally trained in Music, gaining her LRAM. She studied movement under Rudolph Laban in 1953, and has also studied under Lisa Ullman and Warren Lamb.

She has taught students and worked on many courses in Dance and Movement Therapy, and has applied the Laban principles of movement to the psychologically and physically ill and handicapped.

Now retired, Miss Wethered maintains a great interest in Laban Movement and continues her teaching and course work.

CHAPTER 1

THE FOUNDATIONS AND PRACTICE OF SENSORY- MOTOR THERAPY

By Sue Gretton

Introduction

Early Beginnings

In 1906 CS Sherrington published the "Integrative Action of the Nervous System". Notable in setting forth the functioning of the nervous system as a unit, this work together with previous experimental studies on muscle tone, the works of Magnus on postural reflexes, and the works of Pavlov and others, provided the neurophysiological background for the work of the neurologists and therapists of the 1930s. These are the principles still followed today:

- Motor output is dependent on sensory output.
- Sensory stimuli can be used to activate or inhibit motor responses.
- Activation of motor responses follows a normal developmental sequence.

Sensation and Perception

In the 1940s and 50s an increasing number of investigators began to examine perception in the fields of psychology, psychiatry and learning disorders. Perception was defined in many ways, for example, 'an activity of the brain between sensation and thought', 'a conscious awareness of sensations'.

Of great significance at this time, Piaget, a Swiss psychologist, emphasised the importance of an adequate sensory-motor foundation for the subsequent development of motor, perceptual and cognitive skills. By the 1960s and 70s sensory and perceptual-motor techniques and programmes flourished for the remediation of dysfunction in both the neurologically impaired and the learning disabled. The works of Rood, Bobath, Kephart, Ayres, Frostig and Horne undergo constant revision and refinement today, but still have their basis in the works of the early 19th century.

Human Development

The physical, sensory, perceptual, emotional, cognitive, cultural and social aspects of a person contribute and interrelate to make him or her a highly complex being. As the individual grows, these aspects, dynamically interrelated and interdependent, mature and expand along a developmental continuum. Those who work with individuals who have had an interruption in one or more areas of development at any stage of life, must understand the underlying principles of growth and function and sensation and movement, which are predictable for normal human development.

A therapist is an agent of change. A client, often against severe odds, must change and adapt within his or her life situation. As the therapist can directly influence the quality of that change she must know the range and potential for change available, and have a working knowledge of the concepts of change and adaption belonging in the study of human development. The normal must be learnt in order to assist the child or adult with a disruption in the normal pattern of development.

General Principles

Growth and Function

Muscular development, control and co-ordination progress from the head to the feet. Head control precedes that of the trunk and lower extremities. A child must have good head control if he is going to develop other effective motor skills.

Parts of the body closest to the spine tend to be controlled in a co-ordinated manner before the parts farthest away from it. Co-ordination of the shoulder muscles comes before that of the hand and fingers. Muscle co-ordination follows a medial to lateral course of development, from the mid-point of the body outwards.

Initially, most of the motor activity of the infant consists of whole body movement. With maturity these undifferentiated and generalised mass responses become more specific. For example, at first the infant moves his arms freely, in no specific pattern, but within a few months he is able to hold an object in his hand. Mastery of the larger muscles comes before mastery of the smaller. This then becomes very refined and definite, allowing us to acquire fine skills.

Sensation and Movement

From birth onwards we are activated by powerful sensa-tions. These come from sensory receptors in the sensory organs of the skin, eyes, ears, in the muscles, tendons and joints, in the gravity receptors of the inner ear and from inside the body. *Sensory-motor* is a term applied to the combination of input of the sense organs and the output of motor activity. The motor activity reflects what is happening in the sense organs eg. in the eye, visual sensations; in the ear, hearing and gravity sensations; in the skin, tactile sensations; in the tongue, taste; in the nose, smell.

A complete perceptual learning system includes provision for:
- Reception of a variety of types of input.
- The integration of present and past experiences.
- Output in the form of muscular response and continuous feedback.

No area operates independently. Each is influenced and modified by the others. We should not think of input (perceptual or sensory activities) and output (motor or muscular activities) as separate. NC Kephart, Dr. of Psychology, suggests that we think of them as hyphenated, sensory-motor, perceptual-motor.

We learn through sensation, that is to say we do not learn movements but the sensations of movement (Bobath). Activities are learnt through the sensory-motor experience of the move-ment. Co-ordination of movement occurs on the basis of known patterns (using experience and memory of what we have done before). When we initiate a movement we co-ordinate its pattern before we perform it. A child or adult with abnormal co-ordination has neither experience nor memory of normal movement and will initiate movement on the basis of his abnormal sensory-motor pattern.

The development of righting balance and protective extension responses depend upon the correct sensory informa-tion from eyes, skin, muscles, joints, ligaments and gravity receptors from the inner ear reaching the nervous system and activating the response or reaction. Thus the righting reactions, which bring us up in space – the equilibrium or balance reactions, which keep us in space – and the protective extension responses, which occur when one goes beyond the point of balance, are activated by a combination of precise information.

The Nervous System

Over 80% of the nervous system is involved in processing or organising sensory input. The spinal cord, brain stem, cerebellum, and cerebral hemispheres use the sensory input from the sensory receptors of the body to produce awareness, perception and learning. Sensations are processed at various levels of the brain to produce body posture, movements, tone in muscles, and planning and co-ordination of movement. Our emotions, thoughts and memories play an important part in the organisation of these nervous system processes.

Structures and Sensory Motor Functions

CORTEX
The outer layer of the cerebral hemispheres includes areas for precise sensory processing especially visual, auditory and touch sensations. There are also areas for fine voluntary body movements and speech. Some areas are specialized to interpret information from one sense. Each area also receives information from the other senses eg. the visual area processing parts of sound, touch and movement sensations. There are also special association areas which co-ordinate many kinds of sensory experience to give a whole meaning.

CEREBRAL HEMISPHERES
Two large sections which lie over and around the brain stem. They continue the sensory processing that begins at lower levels and assist in producing movement responses. Within the hemispheres lies the limbic system – a set of structures that are involved in emotionally based behaviour.

BRAIN STEM
The upper part of the brain stem is called the mid brain. Through it pass all pathways for movements, all pathways for sensation, except vision and smell. The main part of the brain stem is often referred to as the primitive brain. It is the specialised extension of the spinal cord concerned with vital functions, respiration, heart-rate, body tone, equilibrium and state of awareness. The lowest part of the brain stem is called the medulla.

CEREBELLUM

This is attached to the brain stem and is connected ultimately with the balancing apparatus and cortex. It has three functions. Firstly to co-ordinate impulses derived from organs of balance and from joints. Secondly to monitor all impulses from the brain to check that movements follow the intended path. Thirdly to maintain normal tone in the muscles by acting on the brain stem. Low muscle tone, unsteadiness and incoordination are seen as a result of damage to this area.

SPINAL CORD

This is the continuation of nervous tissue of the brain down the spinal canal. It contains many nerve tracts that carry sensory information up to the brain, and motor messages down to the nerves, which then carry those messages to the muscles and organs. Thirty-one pairs of spinal nerves carry sensations of touch and pressure, vibration, pain, temperature and movement. There is also a set of nerves known as the cranial nerves which run from the head and face directly to the brain – and from the brain back to the head and face, without passing through the spinal cord. They have either sensory-motor, or sensory functions. For example, the fifth nerve supplies the mouth and tongue and operates in the newborn to elicit feeding behaviour. This is of particular interest as it provides the infant with the first sensory experience of his environment.

Lateralization

Most sensory and motor messages cross in the brain stem on their way to the cerebral hemispheres. Sensations from the right side of the body cross to the left hemisphere and vice versa. The left hemisphere controls the right side of the body. Certain functions are specialised in one hemisphere. In right-handed people, the left hemisphere is better at directing fine motor skills; this person will use his right hand for writing. He uses the left hemisphere for language and logical purposes. The right hemisphere deals more with the spatial relationships among visual and touch sensations and musical patterns. Good specialization usually leads to overall efficiency in brain processes.

Reflexes

Reflexes of the Spinal Cord, Brain Stem and Cortex

The nervous system has been built up from relatively primitive structures, represented by the spinal cord and the lowest part of the brain stem. These structures are capable of simple, crude and unvarying movements or reflexes, on to which have been built progressively more complex systems of movement. This has enabled the organism to refine the simple movements of the early reptiles, increasing the possibilities of choice of movement under varying circumstances. The higher centres of the nervous system, represented by the brain and upper part of the brain stem, are anatomically more complex than the lower centres.

Movements can be regarded as evolving from simple invariable spinal reflexes to more elaborate patterns of movement depending on the higher centres that have been added in the course of evolution.

The most humble functions such as withdrawal from pain, are the simplest and the most rigidly organised, in the sense that a given stimulus can only produce a specific given response. They are least susceptible to disruption. Only a complete severance of their motor pathways will stop these reflexes from occurring. The higher motor functions can be seen to be the least organised because they bestow an element of choice, but they are more easily disorganised.

In general when a motor system is damaged the most primitive reflexes remain intact, while the more delicate and complex movements are disrupted. The child or adult can only express himself in a limited motor pattern, being deprived of the vast repertoire of a normal motor system.

The simplest of all reflexes is the stretch reflex. As its name implies it describes the automatic contraction of a muscle when stretched, due to impulses generated in the muscle and carried to the motor cells of the spinal cord. They are of two kinds: phasic, brought about by rapid stretching (eg: knee jerk); and tonic, brought about by more gradual stretch.

Spinal movements are essentially movements of flexion and extension, but above the spinal centres are centres in the brain stem which impose upon the spinal mechanisms more general postures and more complex movements. Before describing the brain stem reflexes it is important to discuss *tone*. Normal postural tone is essential if normal movements are to be carried out. All disorders of co-ordination are associated with disorders of tone. The basis of all tone is the flow of impulses from specialised sensory receptors inside the muscles, in the joints of the neck and also in the inner ears. In the muscles these sensory receptors are in effect feelers of length and tension. Similarly in the inner ears receptors sense gravity, acceleration and deceleration. Both sets of sense organs, in conjunction with touch stimulation of the body, feed information continually into the central nervous system. The function of muscle tone is to maintain posture and balance. Postural tone must be high enough to support the person in a functional upright antigravity position, but low enough to allow movement to occur while the individual is upright. It is upon the distribution of postural tone that the brain stem reflexes act.

The brain stem reflexes concerned with postures are:
- The tonic labyrinthine reflexes
- The tonic neck reflexes
- The neck and body righting reflexes
- The startle reaction

These all interact with one another in normal development, and with other complex motor patterns outside the brain stem (see cortical reflexes). Reflexes that help to govern the distribution of postural tone are referred to as the Tonic Reflexes. They include the tonic labyrinthine and tonic neck reflexes, the associated reactions and the positive and negative supporting reactions.

The tonic labyrinthine reflex is brought about by changes of the position of the head in space, and originates in the inner ear. This reflex governs tone, and is commonly seen in the child with cerebral palsy. When lying on his back strong extensor tone prevents him from raising his head and sitting up and from pulling himself up using his arms. He is prevented from bringing his arms together in mid-line positions, deprived of exploring and touching his own body, and hand to mouth activity. When lying on his front the child is trapped by increased flexor tone – he cannot raise his head, free his arms from under his body and cannot get on to his knees. In less severe cases the child may make compromises between extensor and flexor tone, gaining for example sitting or standing balance at a loss of normal posture.

The asymmetrical tonic neck reflex is brought about by turning of the head and originates in the muscles and ligaments of the neck. This results in increased extensor tone in the limbs on the side to which the head is turned, and flexor tone in the opposite side. In the cerebal palsy child this may prevent him from grasping an object while looking at it, bringing his hand to his mouth, and following an object across the mid line of his body. The reflex is usually stronger on the right side and most children showing this response learn to use their left hand.

The symmetrical tonic neck reflex is brought about by raising or lowering the head, and originates in the neck muscles. Raising the head results in increased extension of the arms and flexion of the legs. Bending the head down results in the opposite. The cerebral palsied child is deprived of correct kneeling positions, and subsequent crawling patterns.

Associated reactions are tonic reactions acting from one limb on the other. These can be seen in normal people during times of physical stress, for example when lifting something heavy. If a hemiplegic client grasps and squeezes a ball placed in his normal hand, increased tone will show in the opposite hand, accentuating the hemiplegic posture.

The positive supporting reaction makes the lower limb rigid for weight-bearing purposes. We are more aware of this when standing on one leg. It is brought about by touching the ball of the foot on the ground and by pressure resulting in a stretch of the small muscles of the foot. If a spastic child puts his foot to the ground he is often prevented from standing by increased extensor spasticity. When he stands at all it will be on the front of the foot with the legs turned inward and pulled towards the mid-line of the body. This makes the standing base narrow and any walking pattern abnormal.

Tonic reflexes are most obvious at specific stages of development during infancy. They remain with us throughout life and are evident at times of stress or fatigue. As previously discussed they are seen to dominate tone in the brain-damaged child or adult. Knowledge of the tonic reflexes helps us to recognise the influence of each postural reflex on the co-ordination of posture and movements.

The neck and body righting reflexes are important in laying down the foundations of normal movement. They allow the baby to move from the horizontal gravity-dependent position at birth to the controlled upright position of the adult. They help to align the head vertically against gravity. This becomes our visual point of reference for body movements for the rest of life. The righting reactions bring about body control in mid-line positions which must be present before movements across the body mid-line can develop.

Equilibrium reactions are the last movement-orientated reflexes to emerge in the developing infant. They develop when the infant has practised all possible movement combinations using the righting reactions. The child is able to maintain activity against gravity. This frees the arms from body support, allows the child to stand and walk in a well co-ordinated fashion and to develop finer hand control.

Cortical reflexes of interest include the following:-

• The grasp reflex is an exploratory reaction brought about by contact with the palm of the hand, or stretching the fingers. It is present at birth but fades after a few weeks.

• The tactile-avoiding reaction is discriminative in nature and is brought about by light contact on the back of the hand or forearm. It develops later than the grasp reflex but quickly disappears. If it is increased the limb is folded in towards the body with the elbow flexed. This is a characteristic posture – seen in some cases of cerebral palsy.

• The placing reaction of the legs is caused by touch sensations on the upper part of the foot and the front of the lower leg brought about by making contact with the table's edge. A baby held gently under the arms in this manner will seemingly step on to the table by raising his foot above the table, straightening the leg and placing the foot firmly on the table top.

Implications

In addition to increasing our understanding of normal movement, knowledge of reflexes can aid in the diagnosis of deviant or abnormal motor behaviour in an infant, child or adult, and may allow for prognostication of future motor function. We use our knowledge of reflexes to determine a developmental age in infants and a chronological age in premature infants. Some reflexes are consistently symmetrical in nature and fairly easy to elicit in the infant of proper age, for example the Moro or Startle reaction. Consistent asymmetrical responses in those reflexes could indicate an orthopaedic problem (eg. fracture), a peripheral nerve injury (eg. Erbs palsy), or a central nervous system lesion, such as hemiplegia. Abnormality may also be expressed by failure of a given reflex or set of reflexes to develop or occur at the age when they are normally easy to obtain upon testing. These could include any of the primary reflexes and the later righting and equilibrium reactions.

Finally and of tremendous importance is the simplest of all the reflexes — the stretch reflex; if the stretch reflex is abnormal, then the other reflexes will be abnormal. Reflexes most commonly associated with an abnormal stretch reflex are the tonic reflexes. The extent of reflex patterns which appear after injury reflect the severity of damage to higher centres of the brain. Predominance of a large number of primitive patterns of reflex movement may indicate extensive damage.

The Senses

Without a good supply of many kinds of sensation the nervous system cannot develop adequately. Every sensation is a form of information; the nervous system responds to this input and produces responses which adapt the body and mind to the information.

Touch or Pressure (tactile sense)

In skin: sensations of pressure, touch, vibration and tickle. The tactile system is the largest sensory system and is the first to develop in utero. Sensations are of two types, specific, and non-specific: the processing of precise information from the hand, face and mouth area is seen as specific, and the maintenance of the balance of excitatory and inhibitory forces throughout the body as non-specific.

Special cells in the brain stem process protective and discriminative sensations, for example, pain, temperature, wetness and texture. Location of sensation and discrimination of shape are processed in the sensory areas of the cerebral cortex.

Touch sensations flow through the entire nervous system and influence every neural process to some extent. Touch is very important to overall neural organisation — without enough tactile stimulation the nervous system tends to become unbalanced. Before an individual can gain meaning from tactile stimuli he must be able to inhibit the protective type of response. This comes about as a result of touch pressure stimulation of skin receptors. Any part of the body surface which does not receive normal tactual stimulation will develop a protective as opposed to a discriminative or perceptive response. The ticklish child has this inclination. The tendency to react defensively to touch sensations is termed 'tactile defensiveness'. A child with this problem does not seem able to inhibit the protective type of response. Many sensations make him feel uncomfortable — touching and being touched, clothing, food in the mouth, different surfaces and textures. Everyday activities such as bathing, cutting his nails and using paste and paint in school may lead to distress, and in some cases catastrophic behaviour.

Dr Harry F Harlow, having studied the behaviour of infant monkeys, concluded that comfortable touch sensations were a critical factor in the infant's emotional attachment to his mother and in the ongoing development and organisation of the emotional processes of the brain. Infant monkeys deprived of maternal sensory stimulation grew up to have severe disorders and showed much of the stimulus-seeking behaviour seen in the institutionalized child or adult. Touching and being touched have an important influence on the infant for the rest of his life.

We know that cuddling and rocking will comfort a crying baby. It is also likely that holding and touching the baby helps him to develop and organise sensation.

A child or adult with difficulty in locating, discriminating and identifying things he touches or things that touch him is usually receiving only vague incoming information. This will affect his response in outgoing direction, much like trying to write with a mitten on the hand. Good tactile processing contributes to the development of body awareness, planning of movement and ability to co-ordinate the two sides of the body.

Temperature

Functions of receptors include conscious sensation of temperature and regulation of the body temperature.

Pain

Receptors in skin, tissues, bones, joints and in the internal organs respond to varying types of pain stimuli. Superficial pain derives from skin, deep pain from muscles, bones, joints and internal organs. Superficial pain can be elicited by pinching or pricking the skin. Deep pain is usually elicited by cramp or headache and visceral pain from stomach ulcer and gall stones. Subjective though it is, a verbal description often provides crucial evidence of underlying disease.

Pain sensations obviously activate the defensive system, but deep pressure sensations tend to modulate or inhibit it. Techniques of inhibition and stimulation are used in therapy and in everyday life. We use deep pressure when rubbing our shin or elbow when we have knocked it, to modulate the pain sensation.

Taste (gustatory sense)

This requires the substance tasted to be in solution and is restricted to the tongue and palate. The different taste buds are receptive to particular tastes, sweetness, saltness, sourness and bitterness. The different types of taste buds are found on specific regions of the tongue.

Smell *(olfactory sense)*

This does not require the substance to be in solution, and is restricted to the upper regions of the nasal cavities. Many flavours are smelt rather than tasted. Unpleasant smells can elicit protective reflexes. Familiar odours can affect our moods or evoke strong emotions.

Proprioception

The sensations from one's own body include sensations of movement, direction, velocity of movement and sense of position. They are referred to as proprioceptive sensations, "proprius" meaning "one's own". The proprioceptive system is almost as large as the tactile system. Proprioceptive sensations are caused by contracting and stretching the muscles, by bending, straightening, pulling, or compressing the joints between bones, and by the movement of the ligaments over joints and bones.

Sensations pass up the spinal cord to the brain stem and cerebellum and some reach the higher centres. We rarely notice the sensations of muscles and joints unless we deliberately pay attention to our movements. This is because they are processed in areas of the brain that do not produce conscious awareness.

The proprioceptive sensations from the body occur especially during movement, but also when we are standing still. The muscles and joints constantly send information to the brain to tell us about our position. With eyes closed or in darkness we are aware of the position of limbs, the orientation of their parts with one another, and the angles at each of our joints. When we have not moved for a long time, or when we wake from sleep, our sense of their position is well preserved. Proprioception assists movement, its fluidity, speed, efficiency and sequence, without the need for visual location of the body parts.

Proprioception contributes to the development of the sensory motor abilities of body awareness, planning of movement and co-ordination of the two sides of the body. In addition it contributes to the perceptual motor abilities of space and form perception and assists the tactile system in giving information about resilience and texture.

Of great importance is the contribution of proprioceptive

sensations with gravity sensations from the inner ear for the development and maintenance of the righting, balance, and protective-extension reactions in the developing infant, and for the maintenance of postural tone.

Hearing and vestibular mechanisms of the inner ear

The *auditory system* is closely related to the vestibular system, firstly by location — the auditory and vestibular receptors being found in the bony labyrinth of the inner ear; and secondly by the fact that both systems respond to vibration. In the auditory system vibrations of particular wave length are picked up by the auditory receptors. Sounds of different pitch are sensed by different regions of the labyrinth. The slight difference in time of arrival of the sound waves at the two ears is appreciated by the brain as a sense of direction of the source of the sound.

In the *vestibular system* one type of vestibular receptor responds to the force of gravity, when the position of the head is moved in space. The other receptor responds to changes in speed and direction of movement giving us the sense of movement. Technically we term these movements acceleration and deceleration movements, although we also respond to vertical, horizontal and rotary movements. The vestibular system forms the basic relationship of a person to gravity and the physical world. The system has interconnections with almost every other part of the brain, and its receptors are the most sensitive of all sense organs.

Vestibular sensations assist the visual system in interpreting the orientation of head and body so that we can gain information from the eyes, for example, to define whether the body, or the object, is moving or at an angle.

Vestibular receptors can give information about the head's position but must rely on good muscle and joint sensations from the eyes, neck and other body parts. If one is passively rotated the vestibular apparatus is stimulated and the visual environment is displaced. This elicits a series of eye movements (vestibular nystagmus) which serve to move the eyes against the direction of rotation of the body, so that the direction of gaze is preserved.

The function of the vestibular system can be tested by measuring the eye movements after a client has been rotated for a given amount of time at a given speed, whilst seated on a rotating chair. This is called testing the postrotary nystagmus.

Strong excitation of the vestibular mechanisms is often associated with unpleasant sensations, dizziness, nausea, sweating and motion sickness. Chronic loss of labyrinth can be compensated for as long as one can orient visually. In the dark the deficit becomes noticeable. Vestibular sensations contribute to muscle tone and smooth and accurate movements. Good vestibular direction of postural and balance responses are important when we are trying to walk on uneven ground. Sensations also contribute to postural adjustments, when we shift our body weight when lifting an object. They stimulate the body muscles to contract in order to prevent ourselves from being pushed over. Lastly they help to save us from falling, and when we are falling to protect our face and chest.

Vestibular sensations are used with proprioceptive and visual sensations to assist in the development of sensory-motor abilities of body awareness, planning of movement and space perception.

Vision

We are able to discriminate visual details of dimension, movement, spatial arrangement, brightness, colour, size and form of objects. In fish and amphibians the visual system is organised to respond only to movement. The vestibular system must function efficiently to keep the eyes on a moving object, and to do so when the animal is moving. The ability to see a non-moving object developed at a much later stage of evolution. Even today when a child is learning to read he will move his finger underneath the line of print. He does this because it is easier to follow his moving finger than to follow the stationary letters.

Vision has become our main means of relating to space, but visual development and function still rely heavily on vestibular, proprioceptive and touch systems. Disorders in these systems will affect the way that we see things, for example a child with poor tactile and proprioceptive processing may find it difficult to colour within the lines on his paper.

appear. The emerging control against gravity results in postural stability allowing the child to sit unsupported and pull himself to standing. Increased dexterity, movement and freedom of movement expose the child to increased stimulation; with this there is a marked increase in exploratory behaviour.

According to Piaget new patterns of behaviour continue to occur accidentally during random movements and the child repeats them to see what results they will bring. The child becomes interested in their effect on external objects and events. This is the beginning of intentional action; it is an important stage as it ushers in the concept that objects exist outside the perceptual experience (ie. a hidden or out-of-view object).

The child learns to feel the nature of distance through the sensations of body movement. As he creeps and crawls about he learns the physical structures of space and with better distance judgements he begins to learn how large things are in his spatial environment. Better sensations of touch and proprioception allow the child to develop finer control and precision grip. Alongside this better occular control is necessary. By touching and moving around objects the child learns that they exist even when he can't see them. This is played out in peep-bo games. The child's favourite toys are boxes and small objects. He manipulates small objects with neat grasp. He has the concept of container and contained.

The final product of efficient co-ordination of gravity, movement, visual, muscle and joint sensations is the ability to stand alone. Not long after the first birthday the child will walk alone.

The Second Year

During the second year of life the child learns to walk, talk, plan more complex actions and perform them with efficiency, building on established blocks acquired in the first year of life. By two years the child can tell roughly where he is touched and to a certain extent direct his responses voluntarily. Touching is not only satisfying but is still an informative process giving the child additional information about objects alongside a visual interpretation. The child develops some sensory awareness; skin sensations give him information about where his body begins and ends. The integration of all these tactile sensations is of paramount importance for the development of hand skills, of co-ordination of the body parts and of movements in space. The child practises countless variations of movement to gain additional sensory awareness of how his body functions and how the physical world operates. It is a time of exploration and exploitation of the environment. Games such as piggyback rides and swinging provide the child with a lot of sensory input from the body and from the vestibular apparatus, giving him a feeling of how gravity works, how different parts of his body move, their interaction with each other, their limits and ranges and uncomfortable sensations. This sensory information combined forms a sensory "picture" of the body. The child can refer to body image when he later needs to navigate body movements. The exploration of space in both a horizontal and vertical plane depends on well organised gravity and movement sensations. Climbing further integrates these with body sensations and visual information. Climbing requires a good deal of sensory-motor intelligence and is an important step towards the development of visual space perception.

According to Piaget the child continues in the sensory-motor period up to two years inventing new means by mental combinations; he now has the ability to picture events in his mind. Experimentation is not necessary. He can try out and discard solutions in his mind. The child now understands visible and invisible and can search for a toy in the last of a series of hiding places.

Concepts of Space

Spatial concepts are based upon height, width and depth; the three dimensions of the spatial system divide space vertically (up and down), horizontally (left and right), and fore and aft.

Vertical dimension is defined by drawing horizontal lines which cross the mid-line of the body, enabling us to judge the height of objects. An imaginary line crossing the mid-line at eye level provides a basis to indicate if objects are located above or below this point in space.

Horizontal dimension defines space in terms of the distance an object is to the right or left of the person's mid-line. Right and left develops within the body and is then projected to objects beyond the fingertips. The internal concept of horizontal space is called laterality. Projection of the horizontal dimension into space beyond the fingertips is called directionality.

The third dimension involves definition of the area which lies behind and in front of the mid-line of the body. We locate and organise objects in space on principles of two and three dimensions.

The fourth dimension is time. It is possible to permanently locate objects in space by indicating where the object was located yesterday, where it is today, and where it will be tomorrow. Stable concepts of time include simultaneity, rhythm, pace and sequence. Simultaneity describes two events that happen at exactly the same point in time. Children first experience simultaneity as infants through the movements of waving both arms at exactly the same time. When one act follows another there is a time interval between the point of origin and the second act. This interval serves as the basis of rhythm.

Rhythm consists of a series of intervals which are of equal length. Rhythm can be observed in acts that require a series of movements involving equal time intervals. Those who have not developed a sense of motoric rhythm find it hard to skip, or walk in a co-ordinated manner. Auditory rhythm is identified in rhythmic patterns and expressed in patterns such as tapping a beat or playing a percussion instrument.

Pace refers to variation in the size of temporal elements that occur within a rhythmic unit. The smaller the elements the more rapid the pace; the larger the temporal units the slower the pace.

Sequence is the organising factor in the development of stable temporal concepts. It shows the order in which the rhythmic units appear on a temporal scale. We remember in sequence of time the order in which auditory stimuli occur, the order of sounds when speaking, the letters in a word when writing, and the order in following directions.

Sensory-Motor Skills

Balance and Posture

Balance is based upon the relationship of the body to the force of gravity. This force or line serves as the mid-line of the body, which divides the body into a left and right side, a fore and aft. The opposing muscle groups on the left and right sides of this mid-line and between those in front and behind enable the child to maintain an upright posture. The sense of balance enables one to detect variation in the body's relationship to the mid-line, letting us know how far we can lean backwards or sideways without falling. Movements are ventures into space which originate at the body mid-line. Movements such as walking, running, skipping and rolling allow the child to explore the relationships between his body and the objects in space around him, providing the basis for establishing stable concepts of space and time. Reaching, touching and releasing objects makes it possible for the child to manipulate and explore relationships between objects. The knowledge gained through movement and touch prepare the child to receive objects coming towards him and push objects away, for example in ball games. Exploration provides the child with an awareness of his body and the space around it. Out of this awareness develops body image, laterality, directionality and eye-hand co-ordination.

Body Image (also referred to as the body scheme or percept)

Body image is the unconscious awareness of sensory and motor components of oneself. It is a postural mode, or spatial image of the body. It is expressed in the ability to recognise and interpret touch and pressure on the skin, the body's structure, its positions and movements, functions of the body and its parts in relation to each other and to objects in the environment.

People also have an image of self which is viewed as a subjective experience of the body and the feeling of it. It derives from proprioceptive and interoceptive sensations but also includes the continuing impression a person has of himself – attractive, unattractive, slow moving, tall, short. These depend in part upon his emotional tone and his experiences with other people, goals, social conventions.

Motor Planning

This refers to the cortical determination of type and sequence of movements. It is closely dependent on and associated with body image. Indeed, the development of each is dependent upon the other. In planning the child determines what he wants to do, what he will move and how he will move. Planning motions requires the child to visualise them first.

Laterality

The internal awareness of the space located to the right and left of the mid-line of the body arises from contacts made by the hand with an object near to it. Comparison of the sensations produced by the joint and muscle movements required to reach different objects, enables one to make a lateral grid which can be used to locate objects positioned between the mid-line and the fingertips. Well defined laterality enables one to move muscles and parts on one side of the body independently of the other side, and to cross the mid-line smoothly with eyes and hands. Eye movements which hesitate or jerk each time they cross the mid-line may indicate a problem in laterality. Positioning work to one side of the mid-line of the body avoids the problem of crossing the mid-line when writing, drawing or building.

Directionality

Directionality is the projection of the internal awareness of right and left that is involved in laterality, into the space located beyond the fingertips. Directionality permits one to relate the objects located in space to the mid-line of the body and to each other.

Eye-Hand Co-ordination

This is the co-ordination of vision with movements of the body or its parts. Children first learn to match the movements of their eyes with the movements of their hands. This stage is followed by the use of the eyes to direct the movements of the hands. Eye-hand co-ordination is also called perceptual motor match and visual motor integration. Children with eye-hand co-ordination problems may have difficulty in the following:

• Using tools and manipulating objects into the required position.

• Stopping and starting at a given point.

• Colouring within lines, drawing straight, curved and directional lines.

• Tracing pictures, shapes, numbers, letters.

• Writing numbers and letters in consistent size.

• Writing on a line.

• Performing the eye-tracking movements required in reading.

Occular Motor Control

This enables children to move the muscles controlling the eyes so that their movements match the movements of their hands during the early stages of developing eye-hand co-ordination. It allows children to correlate the muscular sensations produced by eye movements with the different distances involved in locating objects with the hand. The development of the ability to control and move the eye muscles makes it possible to develop directionality.

Summary

The child uses his sensory-motor abilities to learn more concrete concepts, and to develop perceptual-motor skills. Visual, spatial and auditory langague skills coupled with successful mastery of the body and environment foster feelings of adequacy in the child.

Perceptual-Motor Skills

Visual Discrimination

This includes the ability to recognise and differentiate colours, patterns, shapes, sizes, positions and texture, making it possible to identify, sort and classify objects. Discrimination also involves the ability to recognise an object or picture when part of it is missing, to focus on relevant aspects and to tune out irrelevant background stimuli. For example, in a picture a figure is seen to be in the front and the ground appears to be behind the figure – this is called figure-ground perception.

Visual Form Perception
(also called visual constancy)

The ability to perceive that an object or symbol has unchanging properties. This perceptual skill consists of the ability to recognise figures, letters or numerals regardless of their size, colour, shading, texture or rotation in space. Children without visual form perception may have difficulty recognising a figure, letter or numeral when its size, colour or position in space is changed; and also recognising their name if the type or printing is different.

Position in Space

This requires one to relate an object in space to oneself. This perceptual skill consists of the ability to locate forms which are reversed, inverted, or rotated, to recognise likenesses and differences in forms and to discriminate the position of figures, objects, letters or numerals in space. Children who have problems with this skill often find it difficult to:

- Distinguish among directions involving location in space (on top, under, right and left).
- Differentiate among positions of symbols (b.d. p.q. m.w. f.t. 6.9).
- Follow directions involving movement of specific parts of the body to prescribed positions in space.

Spatial Relations

Perception of spatial relations calls for the ability to see the relationship between two or more objects and relate this group of objects to oneself. Children with spatial relations problems may find it difficult to:

• Judge distances between objects.

• Remember visual sequences.

• Copy groups of figures, pictures, letters, numbers, words, sentences.

• Place numbers in rows or columns, as required in arithmetic.

Auditory Language Skills

In order to gain information from what is heard one must receive, organise and interpret stimuli accurately. Those who have problems in processing auditory information may have trouble in:

• Identifying the source of the sound.

• Discriminating among sounds or words.

• Reproducing pitch, rhythm or melody.

• Selecting significant from insignificant stimuli.

• Combining speech sounds into words and understanding the meaning of sounds.

Before a child says his first word he goes through six or seven stages of speech.

From birth	Undifferentiated crying
1 month	Differentiated crying
6 weeks	Cooing
3 to 4 months	Babbling
6 months +	Imperfect imitation
9 to 10 months	Imitation of the sounds of others
12 months +	Expressive jargon
At 1 year	One-word sentences
2 years	Multi-word sentences
and by 3 years	Grammatically correct utterances.

Auditory perception involves:

• *Attending to sounds.* We must listen for and attend to auditory stimuli to gain meaning from what is being presented. We show this by inclining or turning the head towards the sound source, changing facial expression and showing verbal and/or motor response.

● *Locating the source of the sound.* This involves detecting the point in space where the sound source is located, and determining the relationship of this point to the body. The distance between the ears and their relationship to the mid-line of the body makes it possible for us to determine if the sound is coming from the right or left side, depending on which ear received the auditory stimuli first.

● *Discriminating between sounds.* This is based upon differences in pitch, loudness, number, rate of presentation, duration, kind and location. We hear the differences or similarities of the initial or final sounds of words, consonant blends or vowels — thus acquiring understanding for and using spoken language. The sequential reproductions of patterns, or groups of auditory stimuli, in time, creates rhythm. Tapping tasks are frequently used to evaluate rhythmic abilities; the examiner can vary the grouping of the taps, loudness, and size of intervals between taps, or groups of taps.

● *Discriminating between auditory figure and ground.* This calls for the selection of relevant auditory stimuli from the irrelevant — relevant classified as speech sounds, irrelevant as noise.

● *Associating sounds with their sources.* Those who have trouble relating sounds to their sources often find it hard to obtain meaning from sounds. This failure is referred to as auditory agnosia. Children who find all sounds in their environment useful and meaningful except the spoken word are referred to as aphasic.

Summary

Without a solid perceptual-motor foundation the child will have difficulty in learning to read, write, spell, to understand number and to conceptualise. This may affect his work habits and relationships with other people.

Approaches to Sensory-Motor Therapy

There are several approaches to sensory motor therapy. They range from the neurodevelopmental and neurophysiological to proprioceptive neuro-muscular facilitation and sensory integration therapy. Each has a common basis in reflex neurology, but lays different emphasis on therapy. The following offers a brief explanation of the different approaches the reader may encounter.

Neurodevelopmental Approach

In the 1940s Berta Bobath, physiotherapist, and Karel Bobath, neuro-psychiatrist, used a neuro-developmental approach to cerebral palsied and adult-acquired hemiplegics, based on the works of Magnus Sherrington, and others. The Bobath treatment techniques which are appropriate to a wide variety of dysfunctions of the central nervous systems have been developed on the basis of two concepts.

• Brain lesions interfere with normal brain growth, and cause arrest or retardation of normal movement patterns.

• Abnormal patterns of posture and movement are caused by the release of abnormal or immature postural reflex activity.

The aim of treatment is inhibition of abnormal movement patterns with simultaneous facilitation of normal righting and equilibrium reactions and other appropriate normal movement patterns. Abnormal movement patterns are blocked and higher-level reactions are elicited by specific handling techniques, giving more normal sensory experience. A series of graded sensory and motor experiences provide the basis upon which new movement patterns are learnt. Through preparation activities the therapist aims to:

• Normalise muscle tone.

• Provide sensory experience to unfamiliar movement patterns.

• Encourage active movement from the client while still guiding the movement.

• Finally encouraging the client to move actively alone.

Movement is the primary modality of treatment; normal movement inhibits abnormal movement and via normal movements the ultimate goals are achieved. Proximal body parts become the key points of control used to influence the movement and balance of tone in the rest of the body, ie. the trunk and shoulders may be used to prepare the arms for weight bearing. In addition, in order to change muscle tone, techniques of tapping, placing, holding and compression may be used. In summary, Bobath:

- Inhibits primitive patterns.
- Facilitates righting and equilibrium reactions.
- Controls at key points so the nervous system receives feedback from normal movement.

Neurophysiological Approach

Margaret S. Rood, occupational therapist and physiotherapist, based her neurophysiological appraoch on the works of Sherrington, Gesell, Denny-Brown, Boyd and others. She defined her treatment approaches as the activation, facilitation and inhibition of muscle action, voluntary and involuntary, through the reflex arc. Principles of treatment utilised are as follows:

- Motor output is dependent upon sensory input.
- Sensory stimuli are used to stimulate and/or inhibit motor responses.
- Activation of motor responses follows a normal developmental sequence.

An exercise is considered treatment only when the pattern of response is correct and results in feedback, enhancing learning of that response. Sensory factors are essential for the achievement and maintenance of normal motor functions. Skeletal developmental sequences are used to evaluate the patient's level of development, which determines the level of treatment. The use of stimuli is an integral part of treatment.

Therapeutic techniques consist of stimulation of proprioceptors, vibration, rubbing, pressure into the muscle bellies, joint compression, quick stretch of muscle to be facilitated, and vestibular input; in skin, light touch, rapid brushing and ice to the extremities (under carefully controlled conditions). Inhibitory procedures include slow stroking of the spine, neutral warmth and slow rolling for relaxation, whilst wrapped in a cotton blanket, and pressure to the muscle insertion for specific relaxation. Inhibitory and facilitatory techiques may be used together or in isolation, depending on the type of muscle tone and the developmental level of the client.

Proprioceptive Neuro-muscular Facilitation

Margaret Knott and Dorothy Voss, both physiotherapists, utilised and expanded the treatment principles of Herman Kabatt, a neurophysiologist of the 1940s. The technique is defined as methods of promoting or hastening the response to the neuro-muscular mechanism through stimulation of the proprioceptors. There has been a gradual evolution of the technique since the 1940s. Treatment initially utilises the strongest group of muscles and the most co-ordinated movements the patient has. Movement patterns are reinforced by simple verbal commands which utilise the patient's voluntary control.

Neuro-muscular Reflex Therapy

Temple Fay, neurosurgeon, defined neuro-muscular reflex therapy as the utilisation of reflex levels of response to the highest level possible. Treatment is graded firstly by careful observation of the patient's level of development. Existing reflexes and automatic responses are then utilised in treatment, through simple patterns of movement. It is felt that, since in normal development each stage lays the foundation for the next, it is essential that lower levels of mobility be developed before higher ones. Reflexes which interfere with refined co-ordinated movement may indicate pathology. Reflexes can be utilised to develop muscle tone, inhibit antagonists and lead to higher levels of co-ordinated movement.

The work of Carl Delacato, D. Robert Doman and Glenn Doman, is based on Fay's approach. The same patterns of movement are used: sensory stimulation procedures including heat, cold, brushing and pinching are used; vital capacity is increased by specific breathing exercises. Each programme is carried out by at least three adults, because each limb must be manipulated smoothly and rhythmically in the pattern required at least four times a day for five minutes each day, seven days a week. Thus this sensory-motor approach is that of passive movement, superimposed upon the patient – only at later stages is active participation required.

Orthokinetic Approach

The orthokinetic approach is based on the work of *Julius Fuchs,* orthopaedic surgeon in 1920. In the 1950s, Elsbeth Harrison and Ernest Fuch, both occupational therapists, used splints with both neurological and arthritic patients with impairment of voluntary movement, for the relief of pain, and to increase range of movement, muscle strength, bulk and better co-ordination. In orthokinetics, a cuff composed of elastic and inelastic parts is used; the inelastic parts of the cuff provide support and muscle inactivity over the desired area of the limb; the elastic parts provide flexibility where muscle activity is required. Thus the inelastic area is inhibitory, and the elastic area facilitatory. The cuffs are made of elastic bandages or sewing elastic one to six inches wide. The bandages are applied two to three layers thick and left free where muscle activity is required, three to four layers thick and stitched firmly together where inactivity is needed. The cuff is secured with Velcro.

Sensory Integrative Approach

Sensory integration is the ability of the brain to organise and interpret sensory information for appropriate use. It is a primary role of many functional systems responsible for the development of adequate perception, language, cognition, academic skills, emotional maturation, behaviour control, ability to cope with stress, to move freely without fear, and to perform without aversiveness to movement or touch. Because it occurs in the brain automatically and totally unconsciously it is not easily understood. Sensory integrative therapy was developed by *A. Jean Ayres,* an occupational therapist, who approached research with insight from her experiences using proprioceptive neuro-muscular facilitation with neurologically impaired patients. She came to research as an occupational therapist concerned with the relationship of disabilities to functional performance. Her clinical observations include:

● Postural, occular and bilateral integration (including problems with right-left discrimination).

- Praxis, including finger agnosia.
- Functions of the left side of the body (subsequently omitted) replaced by unilateral disregard.
- Form and space perception.
- Auditory language function.

Subsequent revisions of these disorders resulted in the description of a new syndrome, Tactile Defensiveness, characterised by a negative or withdrawal response to certain types of tactile stimulation, in conjunction with deficits in tactile perception, overactivity and distractible behaviour. Ayres emphasised that these syndromes rarely appeared in pure states in any child. She suggested that deficits in any of the specific functional areas should raise the possibility of problems in other areas. Although the categories have been refined and elaborated upon, many of the original test items have been standardised into the Southern California Test Battery for Assessment of Dysfunction (Ayres, 1962). The therapist must know not only how to administer and interpret the tests, but must also have a thorough understanding of neurology and the significant functional systems before planning therapy.

Her principles basically centre around producing controlled and selected sensory input that requires the individual to make an appropriate adaptive response. These adaptions theoretically improve the efficiency of the brain to organise sensory input. Such a theory leads logically towards remedial techniques to facilitate improved integration and organisation at brain stem and mid-brain levels, using sensory-motor and perceptual-motor activities rather than intervention directed specifically towards higher cognitive processes such as reading. Integration of the tactile, proprioceptive and vestibular systems are considered of primary importance because of their contribution to generalised neurological balance and improved perception in visual and auditory systems.

Each child should have an individual therapy programme which should include sensory stimulation and inhibition techniques, inhibition of primitive reflexes, and include activities to help develop balance, occular control and sensory-motor function of the two sides of the body. Although sensory stimulation includes visual, auditory, tactile, vestibular and proprioceptive input Ayres has suggested that techniques for skin and vestibular stimulation at the beginning of a therapeutic programme are particularly effective in normalising sensory-motor function, and therefore enhanced responses may occur.

Techniques

Stimulation	Inhibition
Fast irregular rhythms	Slow regular rhythms
Vibration	Warmth
Pressure	Slow stroking
Tapping	Gentle shaking and rocking
Stretching	Pressure on muscle insertion
Joint compression	Soft auditory stimuli and voice
Brushing	Reduced visual stimuli, soft colours
Icing	Soft textures, smooth surfaces
Resistance	
Visual and auditory stimuli	
Rough textures	

The Basis of Therapeutic Practice

Learning is the function of the whole nervous system. The better the sensory systems work together the more one can learn. In the young child who is still maturing the growth of new neural interconnections may make improvements more rapid. In adults therapy may help them to learn how to facilitate certain messages, and to inhibit others. It can direct information to the correct places in body and limbs, and organise information into useful perceptions and behaviours. Therapy is less directed towards the learning of individual skills, but more towards the organisation of the brain, so that these skills will be learnt more naturally. The aims are:

- To improve the client's ability to process and organise sensory information.
- To provide sensory stimulation in a controlled environment.
- To help to interpret the information and organise an appropriate response.
- To treat in developmental sequence.
- To provide foundations for the learning of new and lost skills.

Sensory-motor therapy approaches are based on the hierarchy of normal development. Emphasis is stressed on the role of sensory input and unconscious learning. Multi-sensory stimuli, as opposed to stimulation from a single sensory modality, is more effective for learning. Programmes are devised to enable one activity or game to provide stimulation in the area of need. These games can be emphasised by the therapist in any aspect that is required.

The rest of this chapter is intended to give the reader a view of some neurological and some psychological disorders seen in adults and children in which sensory-motor therapy techniques may appropriately be used. Although not included in this section, sensory-motor therapy is also indicated for the treatment of auditory language disorders, the aphasic patient, the profoundly handicapped, the deaf, blind, or multiply handicapped child or adult and lastly, for the child in mainstream school with varying specific learning difficulties.

Programmes are suggested of the type that would be used in normal therapeutic practice with each type of client. Sensory-motor therapy requires considerable neurological training. The skill of the therapist lies in her ability to adapt her knowledge to the presenting condition, but above all to the needs of the individual client. It is important to remember that sensory-motor therapy provides only part of the patient's daily therapeutic input; other members of the treatment team include the client's family, home visiting health and nursing staff, supporting agencies, remedial therapists, psychologists, teachers, medical personnel and the doctors who will monitor and co-ordinate the therapy through each stage of the patient's life.

Before any programme can be established the client must be carefully assessed, and a sensory-motor history taken. The following are the aspects covered in assessment:

● Neuro-muscular aspects – these include reflex integration, gross and fine co-ordination and strength.

● Sensory aspects – these include sensory awareness, response to and processing of tactile, proprioceptive, vestibular, visual and auditory sensations.

● Visuo-spatial aspects – these include form perception, spatial relationships and position in space.

● Body co-ordination and integration – these include posture, balance, body image, co-ordination of the two body sides, laterality, crossing the mid-line, and praxis or motor planning.

A general sensory-motor assessment will usually highlight the area or areas in which the client needs help, or may indicate a generalised or more severe disorder such as apraxia. In the latter case the therapist might embark on a more detailed assessment giving insight into the nature and extent of the problem. This case of an apraxic adult client will be used to illustrate this assessment.

ILLUSTRATION

Karen, aged 35, a head trauma client, showed a severe lack of praxis (motor planning) when assessed. General assessment had highlighted her problems to be due to:

● Poor registration of sensory input (tactile, vestibular systems).

● Poor organisation of sensation (body image).

● Limited ability to organise self for action, due to level of alertness.

● Limited central processing and poor selective attention.

● Limited ability to programme action and to carry it out.

A detailed assessment of praxia was carried out. The areas are defined for the reader's information. The activities Karen was asked to attempt are also listed.

Definition	*The Activities Karen Attempted*
Constructional apraxia. The inability to produce designs in 2 or 3 dimensions, by copying, drawing or building upon command or spontaneously.	Simple symbol copying ie. a + spatial relations tasks, block designs.
Dressing apraxia is an inability to dress oneself because of a disorder in body scheme and/or spatial relations.	Karen was unable to dress herself; she knew what was wanted but was unable to plan or carry it out.
Ideomotor apraxia. The inability to imitate gesture or perform a purposeful motor task on command, even though the patient fully understands the idea or concept of the task.	Demonstration of objects without having them at hand. Imitation of same movements as above. Imitation of hand positions.
Ideational apraxia. The inability to carry out activities automatically or on command because the patient no longer understands the concept of the act (eg. using a comb as a toothbrush).	Demonstration of objects with the object in her hand. Series (4–5 photos from everyday situations) Karen tried to arrange them in logical order but became very muddled.
Motor apraxia. A deficit in programming finer movements in the hand, contra-lateral to the lesion site. In most cases the paresis makes it impossible to detect.	
Kinetic apraxia. The inability to blend motor elements into a single, smooth, consecutive motion.	We used a peg-board with grooved pegs. We measured the time Karen took to fill the peg-board (sound side in hemiplegic patients).

On the basis of the assessment, a therapy programme was established and Karen attended daily for ten weeks.

After ten weeks a quick evaluation procedure was undertaken. Karen showed herself able to do the following:

• Copy a non-habitual posture and a series of three postures.

• She seemed able to move in a smoother and more co-ordinated manner.

• She was able to sequence functional tasks on request, unbuttoning, taking off and replacing her coat and cardigan.

• She was able to describe by gesture the use of functional objects; and could discriminate right and left on request.

Examples of Individual Therapies

Cerebro Vascular Accident (CVA)

The effect of the sudden onset of an internal CVA causing hemiplegia, or the shock of external trauma causing severe generalised dysfunction, has a devastating impact on the adult or child and on his family. An adult's physical and mental levels may be reduced to that of a child and a client will need support and understanding if he is to continue to work at this level. He may need to relearn co-ordination of movement, speech, writing, dressing and caring for himself. His adjustment and motivation will be affected by social, emotional and cerebral influences and loss of skills may be accompanied by a change in personality and body image. In many cases the effects of brain injury leave the client confused and disoriented and it is of prime importance to establish a simple goal-oriented routine as early on as possible so that adaption and organisation can occur.

PROGRAMME EXAMPLE:
Low level head trauma client or early CVA
Harry had fallen from scaffolding at work and had

sustained a head injury. He had been in a coma for four days, but was now conscious. He was fed by nasogastric tube. Early treatment aims were simple:

- To help him respond to a simple routine of tactile and taste sensations.
- To overcome fear of movement.
- To become more alert and competent.
- To facilitate balance.

Responding to a simple routine – making adaptive responses to sensations. We stimulated the insides of Harry's cheeks and gums using sweet-tasting lemon or orange clinic-sticks, cleaned his teeth using various flavours of toothpaste and iced the insides of his cheeks and gums with ice lollipops. In order to improve lip closure, drooling and swallowing, stimulation to the face and jaw was used.

To improve feeding competence, brushing, stroking and the introduction of a straw was effective. In brushing a particular pattern was used which stimulated specific neurological areas of sensation. Other stimulation included the use of olfactory, auditory and visual sensations to increase the general level of arousal. Flowery aerosols, jazz music recordings, red lighting and colours were used as Harry's wife had said he loved the smell of roses, traditional jazz music, and that his favourite colour was red. Ice cream, honey and yoghurt were used as preferred flavours. Once his nasogastric tube had been removed, we creamed, shaved and massaged the whole of the face area. (During feeding practice it is advisable to offer solid foods before fluids as fluids are easily inhaled.)

Overcoming fear of movement – by organising sensations. Harry was helped to overcome this fear by learning to interpret and organise sensations arising from the body. He was treated by two therapists and supported with mats, wedges and pillows. The technique involved tactile stimulation and deep touch sensations using cream and massaging the limbs (particularly the affected side for a hemiplegic client). Deep touch sensations are more acceptable than light and give a sense of security. Vibration, rubbing with textured cloths and slow stroking techniques were used. Inhibitory and stimulatory techniques were used to influence Harry's level of arousal, physical and emotional well-being. Sensory-motor patterns, preparation activities and developmental sequences of movement were used.

Becoming more alert and competent, preparing the body for action. Better registration of tactile proprioceptive and vestibular sensations assisted in developing co-ordination of the two body sides, bringing his hands together in the mid-line and locating objects by touch or sight. Better control of his neck and eye muscles, the development of body image and the planning of movement assisted in increasing Harry's level of alertness and ability to use selective attention skills. Movement patterns and preparation activities for sitting, lying and rolling were used.

Learning balance (in a variety of side lying and sitting positions) in preparation for action in space. Simple activities such as pulling a piece of stretchy fabric or a hoop over the head and shoulders (tactile and proprioceptive input). Swaying and swinging and slow rocking (vestibular) assisted in developing better balance and flexibility, abdominal strength and trunk extension. In addition these activities contributed to the development of body image, planning of movement, laterality, and assisted in dressing skills. Activities could be graded in choice of sitting position, ie. cross-legged, sitting on a tilted or wobble board – and in whether or not we assisted him with the activity.

Harry made good progress and in eight weeks was ready to bring himself up in space and to take weight on his legs, and was ready to embark on the second stage of therapy.

Cerebral Palsy

The cerebral palsies of childhood are caused by damage to the developing nervous system before or during birth, or in the early months of life. Consequently the disorders in cerebral palsy are numerous and complex. The principal motor disorders are those of movement and posture, which are seen to separate these cases from the more generalised cases of the brain injured and mentally handicapped child. Associated disorders are those of function attributed to the diffuse nature of the lesions. These are common but are not essential to the diagnosis of cerebral palsy, for example, epilepsy, mental or sensory handicap, speech and perceptual disorders, emotional disorders and poor self image.

MOTOR DISORDERS

• *Disorders of postural fixation.* Coordinated movement is not possible unless the muscles governing the posture of trunk and limbs can be 'fixed'. Impairment of postural fixation is an integral part of most kinds of cerebral palsy. Absent or poor head control, limited vision and exploration, low tone, floppiness and irregular tremor of limbs when movements are attempted are characteristic. In early-treatment stimulation, adaptive positioning (suitable seating) is of primary importance.

• *Failure of suppression of primitive reflexes.* See section on Brain and Reflex development for the development of the brain stem reflexes, and the importance of postural tone.

• *Paralysis and disorders of the pattern of voluntary movement.* Weakness is common to all forms of cerebral palsy. In severe cases it is first generalised, involving neck and trunk as well as limbs, and is often associated with a general physical frailty. The essential features of the weakness are slowness to initiate a movement, crude and ineffective movement, and lack of skill.

• *Disorders of muscle tone.* There are four main types: spasticity, athetosis, ataxia and flaccidity. Abnormal muscle tone is common to all types. Most cases appear to be mixed. It is often more meaningful to the therapist to refer to the type of muscle tone than to more formal classification. Of interest is the fact that superficial and deep tone may be different.

a) Spasticity – also referred to as hypertonus is characterised by high tone. Exaggerated resistance to passive stretching due to enhancement of stretch reflexes.

b) Athetosis – is characterised by unpredictable fluctuating tone, impairment of postural control and involuntary movements.

c) Ataxia – is also characterised by tone which fluctuates usually from low to normal. Unsteadiness is characteristic.

d) Flaccidity – also referred to as hypotonus, is characterised by low tone. It is usually transient in earliest babyhood. Spasticity or athetosis follow.

• *Failure of development of the cortical reflexes.* The reader may refer to Reflex development.

Accurate assessment is essential for functional treatment planning. A correctly selected combination of evaluation procedures is necessary, with reference to the many abnormalities seen in the cerebral-palsied child. No single evaluation tool can be used.

As the cerebral-palsied child suffers from multiple handicaps there will be several avenues for stimulating the child's sensory-motor experience and learning.

The Neurodevelopmental approach to treatment is used with the aim of facilitating the normal components of movement that provide a solid basis for motor development and integration. If these components are absent, primitive patterns persist and abnormal reflexes are dominant. The goal is to inhibit abnormal or primitive movement patterns and facilitate normal righting and balance responses. The therapist uses her own body and a variety of equipment, therapy balls of various sizes, wedges, bolsters, mat, mirror and wobble board. Specific handling techniques are used with the aim of preventing motor responses to sensory input being channelled into abnormal postural reflex activity. For example:

In spasticity movement is used to reduce tone. The spastic child needs mobility with stability in larger ranges and movements. Initially passive elongation of trunk and limb muscles will reduce tone.

In athetosis stability is used in conjunction with movement to achieve mid-line orientation. Firm, steady pressure through the joints is given to steady tone.

In ataxia movement is used in conjunction with stability to increase tone.

In flaccidity weight-bearing is used with movement to stimulate tactile and proprioceptive input. Compression of joints and bouncing is used to increase tone.

Sensory Input includes the use of inhibitory and stimulatory techniques together or in isolation depending on the type of muscle tone and the age of the child. Techniques may be used to help the child gain better registration of tactile, proprioceptive, vestibular, visual or auditory sensations. In addition the child may be helped to integrate sensations from one or more sensory systems during a single activity. Sensory cues are used and reinforced to assist memory development and orientation through familiarity.

PROGRAMME EXAMPLE:

Interweaving of sensory-motor activities used in a thirty-minute session with a four-year-old child.

Kate, a spastic diplegic child (lower limbs affected more than upper), received therapy sessions twice weekly. Recent assessment had shown her main problems to be:

• Impaired righting and balance reactions.

• Marked extensor spasticity in legs preventing independent standing.

• Upper limb co-ordination affected by moderate spasticity resulting in arms being held in flexed position most of the time.

• Slight visual and speech impairment.

One theme of a session was the exploration of the upper limb:

• Tactile Stimulation – stroking, brushing, rubbing with textured cloths, powder, cream on her own and therapist's arm.

• Direction – long strokes, using whole length of arm.

• Verbal – 'long and strong' sung or said in time with brushing or stroking.

• Motor – To emphasise or facilitate extension.

Materials were used to help explore the concepts of length in various ways: paint, to paint length of arm and fingers; plasticine, to roll a sausage and measure it along the length of arm; long socks to pull up over arms; action songs to sing, stretching up arms.

The aims of this session were:

• To give sensory experience to all systems.

• To encourage verbal cueing (speech has a powerful integratory role and can initiate, inhibit, reinforce and facilitate movement).

• To explore one concept, ie. length, in numerous ways for better learning.

• To provide a situation in which the child can learn under his own direction.

Sensory-Motor Dysfunction in Children

A description of one type of sensory-motor integrative dysfunction is described. This is *developmental apraxia* – a disorder of sensory integration which interferes with the ability to plan and execute skilled or non-habitual motor tasks. The characteristics are:

● Clumsiness in motor activity.

● Lack of knowing how to go about executing an unfamiliar motor task.

● A degree of inco-ordination of face and mouth muscles, and control of eye muscles.

● Difficulties with activities such as dressing, building, cutting, pasting, drawing and learning to write.

● Poor awareness of the body and development of body image both in relation to each other and as a basis for the planning of movement.

Therapy aims to provide:

● Integration of sensation at brain-stem level.

● Tactile, vestibular and proprioceptive input.

● Activation of the joint receptors.

● Development of postural mechanisms.

● Development of gross motor patterns of flexion when lying on back and extension when lying on stomach, and cross-diagonal movement patterns.

● A variety of activities to help in sensory integration and better motor planning.

● A variety of types of sensory input.

Sensory-motor therapy is not indicated in seizure-prone children, those with osteoporosis, haemophilia and diabetes.

Before beginning therapy it is important to evaluate the child's level of sensory-motor integration, and to take a sensory-motor history. The assessment areas are gross motor and reflex development, sensation, sensory-motor abilities, perceptual-motor abilities, visual and auditory processing and emotional well-being.

The physical environment in which the therapist treats a group or an individual child is important. The room should be large enough to contain a small group of four to eight children involved in gross motor activities, but not as large as a gymnasium. Part of the floor should be carpeted for sensory stimulation, with padding for exercises. Auditory and visual distractions should be removed. It is important to create a pleasant atmosphere in which the children can have fun.

When meeting the needs of the individual child activity periods can range from 15 to 30 minutes, depending primarily on the child's attention span. A session for example with inhibitory or excitatory and sensory procedures would last from 20 to 40 minutes. A period of general inhibition should initiate each session and may be used at the end of the session to balance a particularly stimulating set of activities. (Lethargic, hypotonic hypoactive children should not participate in these activities as this could decrease their activity and increase the amount of stimulation they require to stay alert.) Daily sessions can include:

• A period of central nervous system inhibition or excitation.

• One or more techniques for sensory stimulation.

• Reflex inhibiting or facilitating activities, indispersed with a selection of gross and fine motor exercises.

PROGRAMME EXAMPLE OF ACTIVITY SESSION FOR A GROUP OF APRAXIC CHILDREN

5 minutes: Self rubbing of arms, stomach, legs, neck and face with a choice of soft or rough fabric.

5 minutes: Imitating body postures – 'Simon says rub your arms, press your hands together.'

5 minutes: Imitating animal walks – with emphasis on the speed and rhythm of steps to be taken.

5 minutes: Eyes closed, guessing, and locating touch. Children sitting in a circle – therapist passing behind children's backs to touch an arm, neck, back.

10 to 15 minutes: Drawing around others and then painting in face, clothing etc. Cutting out shape. Hang up all the cut outs; guess who they are? Who is the tallest?

Mental Handicap – Downs Syndrome

Certain physical characteristics of Downs Syndrome are classic and familiar – for example, shortened limbs and fingers, slanted eyes with skin folds over the eyelids, and varying degrees of mental handicap. Developmental characteristics include floppiness at birth, low muscle tone especially in the face, hypermobile joints in hips, knees and fingers; increased and prolonged tactile sensitivity with poor discriminative ability; sensitivity to vestibular movement. Neurodevelopmental reflex maturation may be delayed, showing in diminished sucking and grasping reflexes, poor righting reactions, delayed placing and balance reactions. As a result of all these characteristics the Downs child is usually dyspraxic. The dyspraxia is based upon poor function in vestibular, tactile and proprioceptive systems.

PROGRAMME EXAMPLE:

Poppy, aged two years, was seen once weekly for individual therapy, and attended once a fortnight with her mother for the mother and toddler group. The aims and activities were as follows:-

● *Normalise tactile sensitivity,* and improve mobility and hand and body skills. The therapist played a variety of games involving Poppy in touching things and being touched. Her favourite game was searching for the animals and people in the sand tray, and bubble bath.

● *Improve proprioception.* Poppy enjoyed a variety of bouncing games, bouncing and being helped to bounce on the mattress. She wore little weighted cuffs and practised walking on her hands and feet.

● *Improve vestibular processes.* Poppy loved swinging and being rocked. She seemed insecure on the wobble board and needed reassurance to lie on her tummy for a few minutes. She felt more secure playing a wobbling game lying on the therapist's tummy.

● *Improve motor planning.* We played games involving copying simple gestures and touching body parts. We played simple rhythmic sequences for marching and we followed hand and foot prints on the floor.

• *Improve co-ordination of the two sides of the body.* Poppy played the rainbow game, crossing the mid-line with hand and eye to make the rainbow arc. We played similar games in many positions.

• *Improve occular control.* We played with the marble race and the swinging ball, following the movements from left to right and up and down.

• *Improve independence.* We played simulated dressing games with hoops and stretch fabric, and made picnics and tea parties for the dolls and teddy bears. We helped them to eat up the morsels of different-textured and tasting foods.

Autism

In 1943 *Kanner* first described the syndrome which he named Early Infantile Autism. He noted five characteristics:

• The inability to relate to people from the beginning of life.
• Failure to use language in order to communicate.
• An obsession with maintaining sameness.
• Preoccupation with bits of objects.
• Evidence of good cognitive potentialities.

Some years later he emphasised these two characteristics:

• An extreme self isolation.
• The obsessive insistence on preservation of 'sameness'.

Two models of therapy are given in this section: interactive and silent. These models differ in both philosophy and approach, but have in common a primitive and basic interaction with the child, dependent on touch and initial silence (gaze fixation and language avoided initially.)

Therapy Models

INTERACTIVE APPROACH

The approach is similar to that described for sensory-motor disorders, but the children's response to the various sensory-motor experiences have to be very carefully monitored. This is due to the autisitc child's limited communication, tactile defensiveness and high level of arousal.

Examples of monitoring in a small group session. Talcum powder was used before cream. Children initially had fun with the talcum powder tins, shaking out the contents, rubbing their hands on the floor and later rubbing the talc on their own arms and legs. This experimenting went on for a number of sessions before the therapists attempted to join in with the rubbing and stroking. Touching oneself is a different neurological process from being touched; it is less threatening as the child is geared to receive the input and the right amount of pressure.

Activities which did not merit interaction by gaze or language but could not be successfully carried out alone were used – being pulled around on a wooden scooter board on wheels, being rocked in the hammock, being swung on the platform swing, and being rolled in the cotton blanket.

As the children became more familiar with their surroundings, the activities and with their therapists, participation in games such as see-saw, facing the therapist, feet touching, hands clasped, were encouraged; rocking back and forth, for muscle strength and better socialization and gaze fixation. Gaze fixation, however brief, was reciprocated, as were any sounds made by the children. The fact that the children were able to eventually accept, engage in, and obtain pleasure from the new activities was a great achievement.

The results showed varying improvements in social behaviour, gaze fixation, spontaneous vocalisations, accepting a cuddle and cuddling, reduction of fear, and the ability to engage in more meaningful activities instead of self-stimulatory behaviour.

Although effective in bringing about some change in sensory-motor integration and motor performance, it was felt to be more valuable a tool for overcoming the barriers of some autistic children, establishing some form of relationship and providing an external source of enjoyment and gratification.

SILENT THERAPY
• Based on the philosophy and teaching of Dr C Ounsted, and documented by J Hobman (see references)
Autistic children appear to be unaware of people around them, to be interested only in tiny bits of their environment, to be cut off from the possibility of interaction, and are commonly seen to

avert their gaze when they meet other children. All social interactions are based upon the act of gaze fixation, and this is implicated in treatment in that the therapist must not try and make the child look at her. At the beginning reciprocal shyness on the part of the therapist will enable contact to be made. Autistic children are seemingly mute and deaf. It is thought that their very high state of cortical arousal limits sensory inputs to a single sense modality, predominantly vision. There is physiological evidence from animals that high excitation narrows the scope of attention; E.E.G. recordings give us direct evidence of the autistic highly aroused state. A high state of arousal limits the child's activity and exploratory behaviour. Novelty and change in routine or environment, positive interaction, or a forced learning situation may further overload the cortex, and the child may display catastrophic behaviour, and undirected aggression.

Organisation is seen to occur when the child is at rest or alone. Therapy takes place in a pleasant room devoid of stimuli, objects and colour. The therapist aims to provide a predictable routine, preservation of sameness, lack of positive or forceful interaction, and avoidance of social intrusion in voice, gaze, gesture and distance from the child.

The therapist and child share these conditions of sameness and simplicity on a daily basis for one hour. Contact is made firstly with the environment as the child touches the toys (which have been placed in a box for him) or the simple smooth furnishings of the room. The initial relationship between the therapist and child is founded upon sameness, reciprocal shyness and the intimacy that silence affords. A relationship is established when the child touches the therapist for the first time and is usually cemented when the child allows the therapist to touch him.

It is difficult to measure and understand the exquisite care with which each new step is taken. Progressive steps can only be judged by the therapist as she learns to recognise the child's minutest reactions to the environment and the response shown to her, eg., a fleeting gaze, the acceptance of a feeding bottle, or the first heard giggle of a child cradled in a bean bag chair.

Blindness

The development of the tactile system is of prime importance to the blind. Organisation of proprioceptive, vestibular and visual sensations normally provides the basis for achieving correct posture and balance. Failure of the visual vestibular mechanism results in motor and perceptual motor problems.

CASE EXAMPLE:

Mary, aged 30, congenitally blind, had failed on two occasions to achieve a level of competence in adult blind training schemes. An evaluation of her problems revealed a strong perceptual motor component:

- Fear when negotiating a staircase.
- Inability to establish necessary rhythms in walking.
- Inability to cross the body's mid-line with the cane.
- Poor perception of physical layout of a room.
- Lack of co-ordination of finger movements in typing.
- Difficulty in discriminating braille dots.
- Poor motor planning in simple assembly tasks, and organising daily tasks.

Perceptual-motor training was geared towards the development of balance posture flexibility, accuracy of movement, rhythm, co-ordination, awareness of the body and its relationship to objects in space. The use of activities to provide and control sensory input especially from tactile vestibular and proprioceptive systems noticeably affected changes in tolerance of movement, balance reactions, postural security, bilateral integration and improvement in performance of skills that directly depended on an integration of those functions.

Summary

It is hoped that the reader has been able to use the building blocks of this chapter to lay down a neurophysiological foundation and to build upon it an understanding of the development of sensation, movement and perception. Sensory-motor techniques have a direct influence on the Central Nervous System. For this reason it is important to understand that treatment needs to be guided with the background and skill of a knowledgeable therapist. The aim of the chapter has been to promote interest and provide insight into the wide area that sensory-motor therapy covers.

Addresses and Information

TRAINING:
Centre for Study of Integrative Dysfunction (Ayres), 201 South Lake Avenue, Pasadena, California 91101.
Western Cerebral Palsy Centre (Bobath), 5 Netherhall Gardens, London NW3.

SPECIAL INTEREST GROUPS:
Great Britain — Auspices of British Association of Occupational Therapists, 20 Rede Place, Off Chepstow Place, Bayswater, London W2 4TU.
U.S.A. — American Occupational Therapy Association, 1383 Piccard Avenue, Rockville, Maryland 20850.
Research Folders edited by Antje Price, Elnora Gilfoyle, Cordelia Myers, Published under auspices of American Occupational Therapy Association (see above).

EQUIPMENT:
Ayres Equipment: Western Psychological Services, 12031 Wilshire Boulevarde, Los Angeles, CA. 90025, U.S.A.
Blind Kit: Smells to stimulate awareness of 4 common objects, developed by Avon Cosmetics for the RNIB, 224 Great Portland Street, London, W1N 6AA.
Bottled Smells and Tapes for Coma Victims: British Life Assurance Trust for Health Education, c/o The British Medical Association, Tavistock House, Tavistock Square, London WC1.

Preston Catalogue: Camp Therapy, Camp Ltd., 116 Tower Bridge Road, London, SE1.

Take Time Products: Let's Help Children get co-ordinated, 27 South Street, Eastbourne, East Sussex.

PROGRAMMES AND KITS:

Cratty, B., Developmental sequences of perceptual motor tasks. Movement activities for neurologically handicapped and retarded children and youth, Educational Activities Inc., Freeport, N.Y., 1967.

Frostig, M., Frostig programme for the development of visual perception, Follett Pub. Co., Chicago, 1964.

Frostig, M. and Horne, D., Teachers Guide, Frostig programme for the development of normal perception, Follet Pub. Co., Chicago.

Upton, G. (ed), Physical and Creative Activities for the Mentally Handicapped, Cambridge University Press, 1979.

Valett, R., The Remediation of Learning Disabilities, Pub. Feason Belmont, Calif. 1967.

Van Witsen, B., Perceptual Training Activities Handbook, Teachers College Press, New York, 1967.

Bibliography

Ayres, A.J. *Sensory integration and learning disorders*, Western Psychological Services, Los Angeles, 1972.

Ayres, A.J. 'Occupational therapy for motor disorders resulting from impairment of the central nervous system', *Rehab Lit.* 21;10, 1960.

Ayres, A.J. 'Perceptual motor dysfunction in children', monograph from Greater Cincinnati District, Ohio, Occupational Therapy Assoc. conference, 1964.

Ayres, A.J. *Sensory integration and the child*, Western Psychological Services, Los Angeles, 1979.

Bobath, B. 'Motor development. Its effect on general development and application to the treatment of cerebral palsy', *Physiotherapy,* Eng. 57.526.32, 1971.

Bobath, K. 'The motor deficit in patients with cerebral palsy', *Clinics in Developmental Medicine* No. 23, 1969.

Brunstromm, S. *Movement therapy in hemiplegia: a neurophysiological approach,* Harper, and Row, New York, 1970.

Freedman, S.J. 'Perceptual changes in sensory deprivation', *Journal of nervous and mental disease,* 1961.

Fulton, J.F. *Physiology of the nervous system,* Oxford University Press, New York, 1951.

Gessell, A. *Developmental diagnosis* (3rd ed.) Hagerstown, Md., Harper and Row, 1974.

Gessell, A. *The first five years of life,* Harper and Row, New York, 1940.

Held, R. 'Plasticity in sensory motor systems', *Scientific American,* 213, 84-98, 1965.

Kephart, N.C. 'Perceptual motor aspects of learning disabilities', *Exceptional Child,* 21, 201-206, 1964.

Kephart, N.C. *The slow learner in the classroom* (2nd ed.), Charles E. Merrill, Columbus, Ohio, 1971.

King, L.J. 'Toward a science of adaptive responses', *American Journal of Occupational Therapy,* 32, 429-437, 1978.

Knott, M. & Voss, D.E. *Proprioceptive neuromuscular facilitation,* 2nd ed., Harper and Row, New York, 1968.

Lovas et al. 'Selective responding by autistic children to multiple sensory input', *Journal of abnormal psychology,* Vol. 77, 1971.

McKeith, R.G. 'The motor deficit in patients with cerebral palsy', *Clinics in Developmental Medicine,* No. 23, 1969.

Ounsted, C. 'Autistic children', *Journal of occupational therapy,* Sept. 1967.

Piaget, J. *The psychology of intelligence,* Harcourt Brace World, New York, 1959.

Piaget, J. *The origins of intelligence in children,* International Universities Press, New York, 1952.

Rood, M. 'Priniciples of the Rood treatment', presented at Horizons in Health Seminar, May 1967 (from material presented by A.J. Huss in Sensorimotor Workshop, University of Minnesota, 1973.)

Whitlock, J. *Occupational Therapy in Rehabilitation,* ed. E.M. Macdonald, — Chapter Autistic Children, Pub. Baillière Tindall, 4th ed., 1976.

CHAPTER 2

PSYCHOMOTOR THERAPY

By Sylvie Barwick

Editor's Note

Psychomotricity is a European philosophy which has resulted in the scientific practice of psychomotor therapy. Although varying between countries, the concept of mind and body interdependence forms the basis for all approaches.

The following chapter presents psychomotor therapy as practised in France. Until recently, the emphasis has been upon the developing child. The use of psychomotor therapy with adult and elderly disorders is now becoming generally accepted.

Since the author has worked only with children, much of this chapter is related to that experience. However, reference is made to the application for adults, the elderly and some specific conditions. Psychomotor therapy, a postgraduate University training, has a developmental basis but refers to the problems of all ages.

The possibilities of psychomotor therapy are very wide. This chapter aims to introduce the French interpretation of this widely accepted European concept.

Lorraine A. Burr

"Psychomotor therapy acts on the body of the child or adolescent through movement. Its aim is for the body to be experienced and mastered; then integrated and orientated in space; finally made ready to meet others and to enter into dialogue with them."
SUZANNE NAVILLE

"Psychomotricity is the conception of motricity when relating to others and the environment."

G. SOUBIRAN

"Our body is a language. A language of gestures, of mimics, of attitudes and of behaviour. Clear and harmonious language occurs when the spirit and the personality have succeeded in developing normally, and in finding their balance. Confused, deviated and inhibited language occurs when the spirit and the personality suffer from various disorders such as inadaptation and uneasiness. Better than words, the body knows how to express internal and deep tension. This is the language the psychomotor therapist tries to free via psychomotor therapy, a therapy which uses techniques such as corporal expression, mime, graphomotors and drawing workshops, relaxation therapy, etc. The psychomotor therapist is then the mediator who helps others to find the keys to their bodies, which leads to the fulfilment and opening up of a balanced personality."

"Psychorééducateur: un métier d'équilibre"
Information leaflet printed by the ISRP (Institut Supérieur Privé de Rééducation Psychomotrice)

Brief History of Psycho-motricity in France

Psychomotricity was constituted because of a practical necessity: through the observation of motor disorders that were not caused by neurological lesions.

Such disorders appeared to be not only an alteration of the motor function but also the expression of psychological and affective disturbances confirming the unity between 'psyche' and 'soma'. Thus psychomotricity aims at re-using this dichotomy within man. It positions itself at the crossroads between other specialists whose approaches only concern one side of man. It treats both 'mind' and body.

In France the psychomotor movement was started in 1947 in a Paris hospital under the influence of Professor Ajuriaguerra, Dr Jolivet, Dr Berges, Mme G. Soubiran and Professor Zazzo. The same team of people started the first course in psychomotor therapy in 1956.

Later on other names were associated with psychomotricity; those of Mme Ramain, of Dr Leboulch and his psychocinetic method, of Pick and Vayer, of M. Stamback, and others.

1963: the Ministry of Education created a Certificate in Psychomotor Re-education. ("Certificat de Capacité en Rééducation Psychomotrice"). The profession was from then official.

1972: Mr. J. Chaban Delmas proposed by statutory order the creation of a state degree in psychomotor therapy under the aegis of the Ministry of Education. His proposal was interrupted by changes in government policy.

1974: a statutory order from the Health Ministry created a "Psycho re-educator" State Degree. This controversial official appelation was to replace the more accurate and commonly used name of the profession i.e. psychomotor therapist.

1974, 1975, 1976: several ministerial decrees were published by the Health Ministry and by the Office of the Secretariat of State fixing:

i the modality of the studies and the curriculum

ii the modality for the first-year competitive examination.

iii The conditions of attribution of the state degree by equivalence.

1980: a decree relative to the statute of Psycho-Re-educators practising in hospitals was promulgated. It enabled the recruitment of psycho-re-educators in the obstetric gynaecology, endocrinology and cardiology departments within hospitals as well as in day hospitals and homes for the elderly

Psychomotricity: Theoretical Basis

The Concept of Psychomotricity

Unlike most other medical or psychological professions whose approach tends to consider either physical *or* psychological symptoms, psychomotricity concerns the progressive development of both the psyche and the soma and their interaction under the influence of organic maturation and social stimuli. It considers the individual in his psychosomatic entirety thus rejecting the traditional dichotomy between 'mind' and body stemming from cartesian philosophy. It reunites man within himself and observes him in action with his environment. It aims at building an individual whose healthy psychomotor development reflects his mental and physical ease and harmony.

The Psychomotor Development of the Child

At birth the child possesses potential that can only be fulfilled and realised if he is submitted to the appropriate stimulations and experiences at the right stages of his development.

The accomplishments of a three-year-old child are considerable. He possesses all the essential neuromotor co-ordinations: he can walk, run, jump, speak, play. He can also discriminate good from evil – such acquisitions are the result of a progressive organic maturation but also the result of personal experience. They have been obtained gradually by exploration of the environment via various forms of movement: mouthing, touching, manipulating, walking, falling, etc. According to Koupernik the corticalisation of the brain itself "is a function of the experiences, and the actions of an individual". This association between organic maturation and neuromotor experience has been described by Wallon; for him the child's psychomotor development follows different stages during which the motor dynamism is linked to the mental activity and the emotions:

(i)   Stage of motor impulses – For the infant, actions are reflex and movements automatic. There is no intention of action.

(ii) Emotive stage – The first emotions express themselves through the muscular tonus and the postural function. Situations are experienced in relation to the feelings they induce and not for themselves. (The interaction between emotions and motor development can already be seen here.)

(iii) Sensorimotor stage – Corresponds to the co-ordination of various perceptions and to the first neuromotor co-ordinations (walking, speech, etc.).

(iv) Projective stage – The child's movements become intentional and directed towards the objects or persons he is interested in.

During all these stages, the motordynamism is closely linked to the mental activity and there is a close parallel between psyche and motricity which will persist throughout the development of the child.

After the first three years and with the beginning of the myelination, motor, neuro-sensorimotor activities are realised rapidly: the child becomes aware of his own body, establishes his lateral dominance, uses his body as a reference mark and is able to adapt to the environment.

Conditions for a positive and harmonious psychomotor development

In order to achieve a harmonious psychomotor development the child must be physically sound, receive the right stimulations, and gain the right experiences at certain stages of his development. He must also grow within an emotionally balanced environment in order to develop a positive attitude when relating to others. There are therefore two aspects in psychomotor therapy: physiological and psychological. Symptoms occur on both sides. If the child's psychomotor experiences are restricted for one reason or another, his development will be hampered and delayed, and psychomotor disorders will arise. Emotional and inter-personal relationship problems usually develop parallel to the psychomotor difficulty.

Psychomotor Therapy

Psychomotor therapy aims at improving psychomotor disorders. In a restricted meaning the term psychomotor is applied to disorders in which muscular activities are affected by cerebral disturbance. In practice the meaning of psychomotor disorders widens considerably; psychomotor therapy could be defined as a therapy aiming at improving the relationship of an individual with the outside world. What is treated is not the organic structure of a function but the function in its realisation and adaptation within the environment. The psychomotor therapist is the specialist of the body in action and in relation to its environment. He studies how an individual uses his body to:
- sense and express his feelings
- orientate himself in space and in connection with objects and people
- act on the world.

He is not interested in the symptom of handicap as such, but in the way the patient experiences and lives with it; in the way he expresses his psychological sufferings in relation to his problems. He also studies how man's actions reflect back to him when his development is hampered. He is concerned with missed steps in the patient's history and psychomotor development; in overcoming a patient's weaknesses, psychological problems and inhibitions. The therapist will help the patient to fulfil his whole personality, to regain his confidence and restore his self image.

To do this the therapist must built up a positive relationship with his patient in order to obtain his trust and collaboration, and to understand him better. A positive relationship is the essential condition for successful therapy.

Treatment of Psychomotor Disorders

In the treatment of psychomotor disorders the therapist will have to approach the patient as an indivisible unit in order to understand the causes of his problems. He will have to consider the following elements:

● the patient's physical body

● the patient's psychomotor development eg. his psychomotor maturity

● the patient's emotional and social development

● the interaction of these elements with each other.

Throughout the assessment and the therapeutic intervention, the psychomotor therapist will need to refer to these factors.

Physical body – the physical body can be impaired at several levels:

● Sensorial level: the person is blind (or deaf, etc) – he does not receive all the sensorial stimuli he needs.

● Motor level: the person is spastic, hemiplegic or myopathic, etc. – ie. not able to co-ordinate his movements accurately; his movements and actions are restricted and he cannot explore his surroundings adequately.

● Intellectual level: intellectual deficiencies may affect the integration of information, the elaboration of the appropriate response (asphasia), the mental representation, etc.

Psychomotor maturation and development – the child has not yet acquired sufficient neuromotor maturity and has not been able to achieve certain basic psychomotor acquisitions.

Emotional and social aspect – emotional and social problems can cause or stem from psychomotor difficulties. If the relationship between self and others is distorted, the perception and representation of one's own image and of the outside world is altered. This distortion hinders the child's psychic growth and hampers his social and academic learning. It can lead to clumsiness, psychomotor instability, inhibitions, tics, enuresia, etc. The functions organising and controlling his relationship in action with space, time and objects are lacking in cohesion, ease and precision.

Interaction of these above elements; the necessity of an underlying method. Therapy is based on the fact that the full development of a human being is the result of many interactions between the factors named above. It is also based on the fact that the first element in the mastering of behaviour is the control over one's body. This is a fundamental law in psychomotor therapy. The therapist knows that any emotional disturbance is expressed through a person's bodily actions. Any discomfort, uneasiness or mental disorder shows through the subject's way of living, expressing himself, moving, etc. Therapy must be adapted to the individual's specific requirements in relation to his history, psycho-organic development etc. It is therefore impossible (and not advisable) to apply strict and rigid therapeutic methods. "Doing so would narrow the therapeutic possibilities and shrink the pedagogical versatility"[1]. The fundamental methods must remain flexible and adapt constantly to the changing needs and demands of the patient. On the other hand without organisation and without method, the observation is incoherent. This shows the necessity of having fundamental method and guidelines. It is with this idea in mind that psychomotor assessment and therapy are divided into the following sub-divisions:

(i)   Body image and laterality

(ii) Perceptivo-motor skills
   • Spatial organisation
   • Temporal organisation
   • Rhythm

(iii) Basic motor skills
   • Co-ordination:
   – General dynamic co-ordination
   – Fine motor co-ordination
   – Hand-eye co-ordination
   • Balance mechanisms and postural control (equilibrium)

(iv) Tonus (paratonia, syncinesia) and relaxation therapy

(v) Psychological and Emotional Aspects (expression of feelings, release of tensions, easing of inhibitions)

Remedial Programme

The remedial programme is based on the results of the assessment and the psychomotor profile obtained. It tunes in

[1]SUZANNE NAVILLE

with the patient's personality, history, social background, family, daily life etc.

The activities are elaborated according to the psychomotor problems encountered (poor body image and spatio-temporal structure) and used as a main medium and thread to lead the therapeutic sessions. Records of each session are kept and re-assessment performed regularly (usually every six months to a year).

However the role of the therapist reaches beyond the practice of corrective psychomotor exercises.

The Practice of Psychomotor Therapy

Psychomotor activities are a medium not a finality. To be educational and therapeutic, these activities must be intentional and purposeful.

They must be repeated and alternated with periods of rest, allowing time for the impression left by the experience to 'sink in' and mature.

A progression must be established based on the ability of the patient who must always be able to understand what is asked of him. Ideally one should only progress from a successfully achieved activity to the next one. As skill and confidence are gained activities can be made a little more difficult. An activity is really useful if the acquired abilities can be transferred to new situations. A pleasant and secure atmosphere must be created in order to eliminate as far as possible anxiety or agitation.

The different fields of psychomotor therapy are linked together. Whatever the specific problems of a patient, all the various sides of psychomotor development are involved, perceptual games reinforce the acquisition of body image for instance.

The room used by the therapist must induce a secure and calm atmosphere and must not distract the patient's attention. It must be well lighted, warm and relatively soundproof. It must not be adorned with unnecessary pictures or equipment. As a rule, only the patient and the therapist are present in the room during the therapy. However, occasionally persons accepted by the patient can become part of the therapy and join in. The patient is not usually allowed in and out of the room during the session. His clothes should be comfortable, and not restrict movement. He can be asked to wear plimsolls.

Conclusion

In conclusion psychomotricity:–

- considers the individual in its entirety and unity.
- considers the reciprocal nature of the relationship between man's ego and the environment.
- stresses the importance of the human and social factors in the development of the individual.
- encourages the child to realise new experiences.

The therapy's main media are movement and the relationship between patient and therapist. Movement is carefully selected so that the patient meets the necessary stimuli and experiences, and learns to exert and adapt his will and thinking to that movement. A positive relationship between patient and therapist helps the patient to restore his self confidence and to express and overcome his problems.

Aspects of Psychomotor Development and Disorders

Principles of Treatment

Body Image and Laterality

BODY IMAGE

Body image – also referred to as body schema – is the individual's awareness and concept of the disposition of his limbs and the identity of the different parts of his body and their connection with each other. It is also the intuition and knowledge the individual has of his body as a whole, either static or in movement, therefore in its relation to space and the environment.

It is a function of the associative areas of the brain. These areas are linked by associative fibres to other areas that are concerned with the reception of sensory impulses and the start of motor impulses. The areas of association are thought to be responsible for the elaboration of the information received by the primary sensory areas and its correlation with the information fed in from memory and other brain areas. They are thus responsible for the maintenance of body image and many other higher mental activities.

For Wallon "body image is not an inborn datum but a physical or biological entity. It is the result and the condition of adequate relationship between the individual and his environment".

For Lebouch, body image is the organisation of sensations relative to the individual's own body in association with sensations from and actions on the environment. The awareness, knowledge and mental images of a child's own body takes an essential part in the relationship between the ego – the 'I' – and the environment. The child has to experience the world through movement in order to be able to build his body image. In this way we can see that our body is the pivot of the world, that we are only aware of the world via our body.

Wallon, Ajuriaguerra and Mucchieli refer to three stages in the development of body image:

First Stage: *"experiencing via our body"* – From birth up to 3 years of age the child's motor behaviour is global. Emotional repercussions are intense and badly controlled. The child learns by means of trial and error thus acquiring everyday praxis. At this stage the imitation of the adult contributes greatly to the psychomotor education. Approaching three years old the child's basic ego is established and he relates to the adult. He has a global mastering of his body but still finds the dissociation of his movements difficult.

Second Stage: *"discrimination of perception"* – (Three to 7 years of age). Motor and kinaesthetic elements are no longer prevailing and are complemented by visual, auditory and tactile sensations. The child is aware of his own body and has a mental picture of it. Approaching 6 years this image is orientated in space. He has, on the whole, more control over his body.

Third Stage: *"representation of our body"* – (Seven to 12 years of age). The child can delay his bodily involvement with an activity. He can 'stand back'.

The acquisition of body image is very important to the psychomotor development of the individual. The organisation of the body image supposes that the child's experiences are not restricted at any of the above stages otherwise his body image will be badly structured or confused and this will lead to further disorders on various levels:

- *perceptive:* deficit of spatio-temporal structure.
- *motor:* clumsiness, poor co-ordination, poor control of general posture and balance mechanisms.
- *affective and interactive:* insecurity arising from perceptive and motor difficulties leads to further problems such as dyslexia, clumsiness, and various parallel affective disorders altering the relationship between the individual and others.

Consequently, in order to re-educate a patient's disordered body image, the therapist will have to find out at which level the experiences have been restricted and develop suitable exercises to suit the needs of each specific patient. These activities aim at giving the patient the opportunity to experience the stages he has missed during his development and involve the levels mentioned above.

In the case of sensory or physical impairment the elaboration of body image is greatly altered. The aim of the therapist will be to help the patient bridge his handicap, and regain confidence.

LATERALITY

The development of lateral dominance is naturally established during the child's development. It is not education, but the dominance of one cerebral hemisphere over the other that determines the laterality of an individual. Such a differentiation happens in the very early days of human development. According to Tournay the right-handed child pays more attention to his right hand as early as 115 days old. His left hand only attracts his attention at the 141st day, eg. 26 days later.

However although laterality is primarily connected to neurobiological factors, social habits do contribute to the establishment of laterality. The more frequent use of the selected side most probably reinforces its dominance.

The ability to differentiate right from left becomes clearer as the child grows older. It allows him to adapt and relate to others and to objects. It contributes to the establishment of body image and to the awareness of the outside world. It also participates in the perceptivo-motor and praxic organisation. Therefore the importance of well established laterality seems obvious. The psychomotor therapist can be faced with three kinds of patients:

- the constitutional right-handed patient
- the constitutional left-handed patient
- the patient whose laterality is confused, not properly established.

This latter group includes:

- constitutional right or left-handed patients with laterality delays
- left-handed patients forced into right handedness
- patients using alternatively their right or left hand for different activities.

Blurred or badly established laterality is the first cause of many a difficulty and can lead to:

- disturbances in the elaboration of body image.
- disturbances in the spatial structure.
- difficulties or delays with writing and reading, dyslexia.

The teaching of writing supposes a good discrimination between the right and left sides.

- such problems are frequently associated with learning delays
- affective reactions such as negativism, various degrees of maladjustment, psychomotor instability, enuresis and clumsiness.

Even in the case of well established left-hand dominance problems still arise. The person has to face neuromotor and practical difficulties. The left-handed child tends to see and write from the right to the left and to shape his letters in the dextrogyrous direction. The difficulties arise because school teachings are based on a left to right education and the shaping of letters is done in a sinistrogyrous direction.

Aims of the therapist are:

- to establish the lateral dominance of the patient and to reinforce and correct it if necessary
- in the case of well established left-hand dominance, to teach

efficient writing habits
* to re-educate associated disorders where necessary eg. space, body image
* to build up the patient's confidence and self esteem.

Perceptivo-motor Skills
SPATIAL ORGANISATION

The body image is built by means of proprioceptive, kinaesthetic, labyrinthine and mostly visual impressions in association with mental representation. Progressively the knowledge of one's own body projects itself to that of one's body in action in space and time.

The child experiences his body as a reference point from which he meets all spatial occurrences. The organisation of a person's space involves good orientation and good appreciation of distance, speed and direction. The concept of spatial relationship regarding others, objects, and time and the concept of spatial organisation, are linked to the nervous maturation but are also the result of personal experiences. Such experiences involve the use a person makes of his body as a reference point or as an instrument of action in space and time. If such experiences are restricted, disorders occur and therapeutic intervention is needed.

According to Piaget the progressive building up of spatial relations is achieved on two levels: a perceptive or sensorimotor level and a representative or intellectual level. Once again, the interaction between motricity and intellectual, mental representation is to be stressed. The acquisition of sensorimotor data depends on the action of the subject on the world; on his experience. Their correct mental representation depends on the ability of the subject to analyse structure and integrate such data. Therefore, providing the physical body of a subject is intact, disorders appear on two sides:
* sensorimotor experiences
* mental representation and integration.

The insufficiency of spatial discrimination and organisation can contribute to the creation of disorders such as difficulties in reading and writing (spelling), dyslexia, etc. Unable to cope with such difficulties, the child may build up a negative attitude, become anxious and unhappy and start to reject school altogether. Behaviour problems often arise and symptoms such as maladjustment, hyperactivity and inhibition may develop; these originally stem from spatial difficulties and may hinder a person all his life.

The aim of the therapist will be to re-educate primarily the spatial disorders according to their origins. He will propose to his patient activities that enable him to realise the basic sensorimotor experiences that might have been restricted and help him integrate and organise such experiences; the aim is to overcome these difficulties and to restore self confidence and a more adapted behaviour.

TIME ORGANISATION AND RHYTHM

Time organisation, like space organisation can be approached on two levels:

• *Perceptive level* concerning the sense of, and perception of rhythm; the perception of a rhythm being the perception of an organisation of phenomenon taking place periodically in time.

• *Mental representation level* concerning the possibility to position oneself in time in relation to past, present and future. According to Fraisse the perception of time is the perception of a succession of events as a unity.

Time concerns psychomotricity because it concerns the efficiency of movement eg. any action takes place in time as well as in space, or in relation to an object. A badly timed movement may be completely inefficient. This concerns for instance the co-ordination of movement; eg. a child must time his action in order to use a skipping rope or catch a ball successfully. Through the practice of psychomotor exercises the patient learns to organise time and adapt to concepts such as durability, succession, speed, irreversibility of time, etc, as must a driver to drive his car safely.

In order to enable the patient to grasp these concepts the therapist will try to translate them in a 'visible' way by:

• association of such concepts to bodily actions (movement)
• multiplying the sensations (kinaesthetic, visual and auditory)
• transposing those same concepts into space
• finally transcripting them graphically to visualise and memorise them.

The progressive organisation of time in psychomotricity can follow three stages:

- *First Stage*: acquisition of basic elements:
Concept of speed (connected with the action of the subject)
Concept of duration can be appreciated in connection with the distance covered (connection with space) or the work accomplished (connection with concept of effort)
- *Second Stage*: awareness of time relationships:
Being able to wait (resist impulses, instability, anxiety)
Apprehend the various moments of time: the right moment, before, during, after and their relationship to each other
To finally understand the concepts of succession and simultaneity.
- *Third Stage*:
Co-ordination of these various elements
Progressive withdrawal of activities using movements and space to use only auditory elements.
Transposition and association to dynamic co-ordination.

THE ROLE OF RHYTHM IN PSYCHOMOTRICITY

A rhythmical succession of movements is easier to perform and less demanding than the succession of those same movements without rhythm as it does not require intellectual effort. Rhythm suppresses parasitic movements, regularises nervous interactions and conveys a pleasant feeling of ease. For instance it is known that stammering disappears if the person affected sings.

Rhythmic activity is economic because of the alternation of effort and relaxation. However, it does not involve the mind as the nature of the activity is to detach the intellect from the execution of the movement. Rhythmic movement is easier to realise because it demands less intellectual effort than the ordinary (non-reflex) movement where fatigue increases with the complexity of the neuromuscular task and degree of concentration required.

AIMS OF THE THERAPIST

Rhythm can bring a certain fluidity, ease and relaxation to movement but can also be educational. Rhythmic activities become educational when the child's attention is involved. For instance, to keep up with a cadence or to materialise a temporal succession and its variations.

However, the main aim in introducing rhythm is to help to

suppress contractures and muscular tensions caused by inadequately controlled movement. Rhythm conveys suppleness, relaxation, and independence of the limbs; all such elements are important for good motor control.

Basic Motor Skills

Basic motor skills such as co-ordination and balance are deeply influenced by the state of our emotions and body tone. Correct balance and co-ordination are essential to the control and command of our movements, for automatic movements such as walking or running and also for more complex activities such as playing ball games, driving a car, etc. The mastering of the whole body is essential to a person as part of a physical and psychological entity. Such mastering depends on the perfectioning of automatisms, the acquisition of better co-ordination and balance. It can help ease both psychological tension (anxiety, negativism) and physical tension (paratonia, syncinesiae).

CO-ORDINATION

The co-ordination of movements involve different levels of activities:

- automatisms eg. walking, running etc.
- movement dissociation
- hand-eye co-ordination
- fine movement co-ordination

According to Guilmain a skilled and well adapted gesture presents the following characteristics:

- precision depending on general balance and muscular independence
- ability to repeat accurately the same gesture several times
- left/right independence
- adaptation to muscular effort
- sensorimotor adaptation
- ideomotor adaptation

When co-ordination is insufficient or disturbed symptoms range from the impossibility to execute a movement, to the ability to realise it correctly but in a disharmonic manner (clumsy, tense, etc). In between range various degrees of inco-ordination. Disturbances of the tonus have a direct influence on movement co-ordination: gestures are stiff, clumsy, jerky. This alters the execution of movements not only in their quality but in their precision, their temporal and spatial realisation. Gestures are too quick, too abrupt or too impulsive. Movement can be either over controlled or just the opposite, excessively free.

Confused representation of the body and dyspraxiae cause difficulties too; verbal requests from the therapist are misunderstood, the patient hesitates and sometimes gets completely inhibited, his attitudes are uncertain and disharmonious. The request 'bend your arm' can become a movement of abduction or tension in various directions. Motion makes things even worse because of the necessity to do simultaneously or alternatively certain gestures; to use the body axis. Then, errors and confusions between the two body halves can occur.

The aims of the therapist are:
- to improve automatisms
- to bring a better control of the intentional motricity, of the command of the body
- to ease movement, thus leading toward physical, then mental relaxation.

EQUILIBRIUM: BALANCE MECHANISM AND POSTURAL CONTROL

Correct balance and postural control are essential for any co-ordination of movement. The more disturbed the equilibrium is, the more it absorbs energy which could be utilised for other actions. This constant and unconscious struggle fatigues the mind and diverts the attention. This explains clumsiness and imprecision of movement, muscle tension, syncinesiae, stammering. It also appears to be one of the causes for anxiety and anguish. There is a close connection between the deficiency of static and (postural) dynamic equilibrium and anxiety. Emotions are definitely linked with the patient's general tonic state and his psyche. "An attitude is also a state of mind" (Vayer).

Several kinds of sensations contribute to the maintenance and modification of the balance of the body; tactile impressions, visual, kinaesthesic and labyrinthine sensations. These sensations must be educated in parallel with the equilibrium reflexes and transferred to dynamic and progressively more complex activities.

Disturbances in the equilibrium occur when the patient's experiences in relation to the above sensations have been restricted; when there is paratonia[1] stemming either from emotional disorders or delays in maturation; when the equilibrium centres have been damaged (labyrinth, cerebellum); when the neuromotor equipment is affected.

The aim of therapy is to establish and maintain an economic and balanced posture (eg. a good static equilibrium) by:

● educating the senses
● improving the basal tonus and releasing the tension through relaxation therapy (in the case of paratonia)
● transferring the balanced posture to dynamic and more complex situations
● building up the patient's confidence, helping him overcome his physical and psychological fears.

Tonus and Syncinesiae

TONUS

The tonicity or muscular tonus is the normal state of partial contraction of a resting muscle, maintained by reflex activity (Myotatic or Sherrington reflex). The muscular contraction generating tonus is called tonical as opposed to the phasic contraction that generates motion. This tonicity has various roles that can be classified as physiological and emotional.

Physiologically our tonus allows us to stand up, to choose and maintain our postures, balance, to execute our movements, etc. Emotionally it reflects our tensions, anxiety, or our state of ease, comfort, etc. Emotion and tonus interact on each other. Wallon describes in his *Origins of the Child's Character* how the infant and mother learn from each other's tonical reactions. The infant's first smiles and cries are, according to Wallon, emotional tonical discharges expressing either pleasure or displeasure. Both Ajuriaguerra and Wallon refer to this tonico-emotional exchange and interaction as the "tonico-emotional dialogue".

Psychomotor therapy is faced with three main forms of tonical disturbances or 'paratonia'.

Physiological deficiencies that affect the tonus

Damage of the neurophysiological structures has occurred

---

[1]PARATONIA: Abnormal state of contraction of a muscle or group of muscles.

(as in hemiplegia, Parkinson's disease, spasticity, etc). The aim of the therapist is to help the patient learn to live with his handicap and fulfil his physical abilities as much as possible. If the physical handicap has caused delays in other psychomotor learnings – such as spatial organisation, body image, etc – then the aim will also be to re-educate those specific disorders.

Immaturity and Paratonia

Paratonia can be caused by delays in maturity which may stem from various origins. The inadequacy of the tonus shows through the quality of the subject's gestures: gestures are not well adapted to space and time, co-ordination is poor, etc. The aim of the therapist is to resolve or improve the paratonia via relaxation techniques. This will in consequence lead to improvement in other areas (co-ordination, adaptation to space) and is associated with relevant specific psychomotor activities.

Emotional Paratonia

Difficulties in maintaining a good tonus when the neurophysiological structures are intact reflects the inner tensions and emotional or psychological problems of the patient. It can also be a reaction to a stressful situation such as the psychomotor assessment for instance. Tonical accumulation when associated with emotional tensions leads to emotional blockage or inhibition. These can hinder or even prevent the subject's action. On the other hand, it can express itself by impulsive outbursts. In the latter case the tension is eased through uncontrolled tonico-motor discharges (psychomotor instability, hyperactivity). The patient can also fluctuate between these two states particularly during the assessment.

The aim of the therapist is to resolve or ease the paratonia via relaxation techniques, to help the patient to overcome his emotional problems and develop self confidence. Emotional tensions can also be released through 'corporal expression', mime, etc. In the case of deep psychological disorders psychotherapy is used parallel to psychomotor therapy.

SYNCINESIAE

Syncinesiae are parasitic movements that enable the therapist to appreciate the degree of effort and concentration used by the patient whilst performing an intentional movement.

They can also reveal the resistance of the same patient to fatigue and indicate the level of his neurological and tonical maturation.

Mira Stamback describes two kinds of syncinesiae:

Tonical syncinesiae are linked with the tonical state and emotions of the individual. They are caused by excessive and inadequate tonical diffusion within a group of muscles unconcerned with the realisation of an intentional movement. Therefore they indicate an abnormal tonical tension. Because of the functional proximity of certain activities, there is infiltration of the tonus in areas which are not concerned with the movement that is being realised.

Syncinesiae of imitation (also referred to as syncinesiae of reproduction) consist of the reproduction of an intentional movement in the hemisphere of the body not concerned with this movement. For instance a voluntary movement of alternative supination and pronation of the left hand will cause the same movement with the right hand. Such syncinesiae normally disappear at about 12 years of age.

The development of syncinesiae usually occurs on the non-dominant side and is somewhat connected with the establishment of lateral dominance. Syncinesiae can be: controlateral, uni- or bi-lateral or axial.

Application of Psychomotor Therapy

Psychomotor therapy is indicated for a very wide range of patients; this is because of its specific approach to the individual as a whole, and because of the verflexibility of its resources. In fact psychomotor 'education' is beneficial to everyone because it improves and perfects automatisms and skills. The therapy is indicated for specific psychomotor disturbances, for emotional and social disturbances and physical and intellectual handicaps. Patients can be treated at any age in their lives: from birth to old age.

The intervention of the psychomotor therapist occurs on two levels: those of prevention and therapy.

Prophylactic Aspects

The prevention of psychomotor delay can be helped by psychomotor education:

BABIES, INFANTS AND CHILDREN

• Sensorimotor stimulation (baby and infant) is indicated to prevent further psychomotor and emotional disturbances for babies showing abnormalities or delays in their physical or emotional development such as: spina bifida, spasticity, cardiopathy, sensory deficiencies, autism, Down's Syndrome, psychomotor delays, paratonia (floppy or stiff babies), passivity, withdrawal, hyperkinetic syndrome, premature babies, etc. Assessment and remedial programme are established according to specific baby charts such as Brunet-Lezine's Baby Tests; Piaget and Gesell's Vision Tests, etc. Passive and active sensorimotor education usually involves the baby's mother and includes manipulations and various sensorimotor activities.

• Prevention of the 'Syndrome of Hospitalization'. This syndrome was first described by Spitz. It develops as a result of lack of physical contact caused by an infant's prolonged stay away from his mother (in hospital for instance). Psychological and physical disturbances occur such as delay of physical development, language delay, emotional disorders (anxiety then indifference), lesser immunity to illness, etc. According to Spitz disturbances are irreversible if the baby remains isolated and unstimulated for over 5 months: hence the importance of sensorimotor education to prevent such syndromes.

• Prevention of disorders or delays caused by affective problems (handicapped babies faced with maternal rejection etc.)

• Prevention of learning difficulties and slowness at school related to reading, counting and writing. (Pre-writing exercises, space/time activities.)

ADULTS AND ELDERLY

• Prevention of industrial accidents (control, accuracy of movement and motor skilfulness).

• Prevention of illnesses linked with stress (obesity, anxiety, sexual difficulties, depression): relaxation therapy and body expression techniques (role play, mime, etc).

- Psychoprophylaxis in childbirth (use of relaxation techniques).
- Prevention of body image and balance difficulties with the elderly.

Therapeutic Aspects

Therapy may be required at any of the previously described levels. The practice of psychomotor therapy must be adapted to the individual requirements of the patient ie. in relation to his history, psychological attitudes and physical condition. It is therefore impossible to apply strict and rigid methods when treating the patient.

"Doing so would narrow the therapeutic possibilities and shrink the pedalogical versatility. A fundamental outline on the other hand is indispensable; it ensures a solid foundation for the therapeutic work". (Suzanne Naville.)

With reference to this fundamental basis, psychomotor therapy approaches various kinds of problems.

SPECIFIC PSYCHOMOTOR DISORDERS
- delay of psychomotor development
- motor debility (motor immaturity), underdevelopment. The patient presents paratonia, stiffness, clumsiness, syncinesiae, insufficiency of body image and spatio-temporal structure etc.
- insufficient motor co-ordination, equilibrium and postural control (tonus)
- psychomotor instability or Hyperkinetic Syndrome (the so-called hyperactive children). There are various forms of psychomotor instability.
- psychomotor inhibition
- body image
- laterality
- spatio-temporal integration and structure
- rhythm

These disorders are usually connected with the following disturbances:

PSYCHOMOTOR DISORDERS IN RELATION TO AFFECTIVE AND INTERPERSONAL DIFFICULTIES
- physical clumsiness
- nervous tics
- stuttering (certain forms)
- enuresis

- behavioural disorders (certain forms of maladjustment, negativism, inhibition)
- psychomotor instability and psychomotor inhibition can also be classified under this heading according to their origin (eg. reactional instability or inhibition).

PSYCHOMOTOR DISORDERS AND LEARNING DIFFICULTIES

Learning difficulties are often linked to affective problems and stem from or are associated with disorders of body image, laterality, spatio-temporal organisation, psychomotor instability, etc. The role of the psychomotor therapist consists of the re-education of specific psychomotor problems but also in understanding the child's difficulties and helping him to overcome them. This is done throughout the therapeutic sessions via a trustful child-therapist relationship and via body expression techniques that enable him to resolve his difficulties, to gain self-confidence and success in his achievements. Disorders coming under this heading are dysgraphia, dyslexia, school refusal, slow learning, and learning delays in literacy, numeracy, etc.

PSYCHOMOTOR DISORDERS IN CONNECTION WITH PHYSICAL DISABILITIES OF THE BODY

A physically or intellectually handicapped person is not able to receive essential experiences as a normal person does. Mental, sensory or motor insufficiencies have hindered his/her development. The psychomotor therapist will mainly aim at palliating handicaps, at using other intact functions and stimulations, and re-educating the perturbed development and the image the subject has of himself. The therapy brings benefit to: sensorial deficiencies (blindness, deafness), motor deficiencies (spasticity, hemiplegia, myopathies), intellectual deficiencies (children with special learning difficulties, mental handicap).

PSYCHOMOTOR DISORDERS IN RELATION TO SLIGHT OR DEEP DISTURBANCES OF THE PERSONALITY

This concerns certain forms of neurosis, psychosis and autism. Persons affected by such disturbances often experience their body in a different way: their body image is often confused or distorted (eg. in schizophrenia patients often experience sensations of a scattering of their body). Their concept of space and time is often affected, concentration is poor, feelings of insecurity and anxiety cause various forms of mental and physical tension, motor inco-ordination and clumsiness, all leading to failure in many activities. The psychomotor therapist can help greatly by re-educating the listed psychomotor disorders. This can also help reduce inhibitions, blockages and stress through relaxation and self-evaluation. It can give patients an opportunity to express themselves through music, body expression, mime, etc.

Practice of the Profession

Two kinds of practice exist in France, salaried (both in the private and state systems) and freelance practices. In both cases the psychomotor therapist works with a team of other specialists such as psychiatrists, psychologists, speech therapists, paediatricians, doctors and teachers. With freelance work the disorders met tend to be of less acute pathological degree.

Psychomotor therapists work in crêches, nursery schools (preventive side), day centres in connection with nurseries and in primary schools and médico-psycho-pédagogique centres (in France), special schools and days hospitals, and after care establishments. When treating adults and the aged, the psychomotor therapist practises in hospitals and specialised units such as: obstetric gynaecology, endocrinology and cardiology; in geriatric day hospitals, in old people's homes and leisure centres for the elderly.

Example of Therapy

Psychomotor therapists treat patients suffering from a wide variety of handicaps. It is essential to stress once again the fact that psychomotor therapists do not treat a patient according to the nature of his handicap but according to his personality, to his symptoms and to the way he expresses his problems. Any form of labelling (eg. E.S.N., epileptic, psychotic, etc) negates the principle of our philosophy, and of our professional beliefs and methods.

It is true that certain handicaps present specific associated psychomotor disorders but because of the reasons mentioned above this chapter is not going to offer a selection of remedial programmes for specific handicaps.

Michael's Case

Michael is 12, diagnosed autistic, and as such presented autistic patterns of behaviour, such as particular mannerisms, dreaminess and withdrawal. His understanding was poor (limited to a few words) and his speech echolalic. He showed a lack of interest towards his surroundings, the staff and his class mates. His complete lack of motivation made it impossible for his teacher to arouse his interest in any class activities. His behaviour alternated between quiet and dreamy periods and being excitable.

Formal psychomotor assessment was not possible but disorders were obvious in the following areas: body image, time and space organisation (no concept of left, right, up, down, etc); laterality not established, emotional paratonia expressing his inner tension.

The aims of therapy were:
• To build up a positive relationship between Michael and his therapist; without this no demands could be made or any work carried out. To help him release his tensions and anxiety and ease out his paratonia.
• To stimulate him and arouse his interest; to involve him more with the 'real world' (eg. in contrast to his own world).
• To deal with the specific psychomotor disorders.
• To help his teacher cope with his restless and sometimes aggressive outbursts of behaviour.

MOVEMENT PROGRAMME
First four months
Hydrotherapy (1 hour weekly)
Most autistic patients greatly enjoy and relax in the aquatic environment (see paragraph on hydrotherapy) and therefore their response is usually better in the water. Michael usually looks weary and unhappy but was a transformed child in the water; he relaxed, laughed and enjoyed himself. Soon he started

to respond to the therapist's demands: kicking his feet, throwing a ball, even accepting a certain amount of physical contact and making short eye contact. Unconsciously he was also releasing excess energy and tension.

Use of music and of play therapy

Parallel to the sessions at the pool, work out of the water was also carefully planned and carried out. At first no demands could be made on Michael, so he came for only short periods to listen to some quiet tunes played on the lyre or the recorder. As he became more familiar with the room, the therapist and his new routine, a certain degree of participation was then asked from him through play (he had to learn to play) and sensorimotor activities:

● joining in actions or games, singing games, percussion games (beating a rhythm, stamping a tune etc)
● joining in simple ball games (throwing and catching a ball to a given rhythm etc)
● sensorial stimulation and education of tactile, visual and auditory sensations eg. touching, feeling and naming objects of various shapes, weights, textures, etc; contrast activities, colour and sound discrimination, etc.

The work and results achieved with Michael during these four months were a spring board for further more specific therapeutic work. By then Michael had built up a positive relationship with his therapist and had become sufficiently aware and motivated to start responding to and joining in with the proposed activities.

FROM THE FIFTH MONTH ONWARDS

Specific psychomotor activities

The remedial programme was designed to improve Michael's abilities in his knowledge of:

● body image: activities concerning the global perception of his body, first spatial data, knowledge of his body as described on pages 92-95.
● laterality, work done parallel to space activities and body image
● spatial organisation: work on concepts of right, left, up, down, etc using hoops and ball games (see pages 95-96) during both ordinary sessions and sessions in the water.

Later on walking and writing of forms (see pages 102-103)

were introduced to strengthen sense of direction and ability to concentrate.

• rhythm and time organisation: the re-education of time organisation proved unfruitful. Michael could not grasp any concept of time. However he had a good sense of rhythm and enjoyed any rhythmic activities. Their use was mostly stimulating and recreational (see suggested activities pages 99-100).

Relaxation Therapy

The activities in the water were naturally conducive to relaxation. Once he trusted his therapist Michael was rapidly able to reach a satisfactory state of relaxation. The disappearance of his frowning and worried facial expression was a reflection of both his physical and 'mental' relaxation. Henceforth, if possible, relaxation therapy was used whenever Michael became excessively anxious or agitated.

RESULTS AFTER ONE YEAR'S THERAPY

Michael had noticeably improved in the following areas:

• his general awareness had noticeably increased (towards his surroundings, classmates and adults) and he was able to carry out some simple commands and little jobs.

• his vocabulary possessed a few more words (parts of his body, directions, verbs expressing movement).

• he showed a preference in using his left hand and was encourages to do so henceforth.

• body image: he could now name various parts of his body and indicate them either on his body or on others'; and he could run, creep, stamp, etc on demand.

• spatial organisation: he had grasped the meaning of elementary directions such as above, below, in front of, behind, left and right, next to.

• general behaviour: outbursts of disturbed behaviour were noticeably less frequent and he looked much happier and relaxed. (His teacher learnt to use relaxation therapy to calm him down and to soothe him.)

His involvement in classroom activities was greater (he made attempts towards writing). In brief Michael had become more relaxed and happier within himself and was now able to make lasting connections with the real world.

Psychomotor Assessment

Observation on Examination

This part of the assessment aims at obtaining details of the patient's psychological and affective development. It is therefore important to obtain as much information as possible and from various sources: parents, General Practitioners, and other specialists and therapists. This is, when possible, preferred to the sole examination of the patient's file.

Such information will concern:
● History and general information: (Pregnancy, age of mother at birth, first milestones, illnesses and accidents, etc.)
● Difficulties encountered so far by patient; previous therapies, reason for the consultation.
● Results of previous examinations and assessments.
● Interview with the patient: this is carried out although most information is already known. However, it is helpful to find out how much the patient knows about himself (self identity).

Physical Development

General appearance and physical disabilities
● Typology (as it influences the general motricity) (eg. thin or fat, asthenic etc).
● Harmony of static posture and gait.

Information Relevant to Tests During the Assessment Situation

● Presentation (tension, inhibition, ease).
● Speech (absence of speech, echolalia, stammering, logorrhea, quality of speech).
● Physical and emotional general attitude.
● Attitude during the assessment and facing the tests.
● Relationship to therapist.
● General development of attitude at the end of assessment (improvement or deterioration of participation and psycho-affective relationship).
● Understanding of verbal request.
● Co-ordination, precision and harmony of movements.
● Degree of tonical diffusion, syncinesiae, difficulty in muscle

and tonus control (participation of unconcerned groups of muscles, exaggeration of movements, etc).

Postural Control and Static Balance

Note that signs of instability of various degrees and meanings may appear such as:
• Real motor instability (sub-choreic movement of limbs, myoclonic movements of neck and shoulders).
• Psychomotor instability, much more frequent, linked with emotional state in reaction to the assessing context. (Restlessness, nervous laughter, tics, tension of jaws, of fingers, etc.)
• Appreciation of ability to remain still standing up, then with eyes closed. Also counting down from 20 to 1 with eyes closed and arms extended.
• Reaction to being pushed by the therapist (regulation and adaptation of postural control).
• Standing on one foot: begin feet together then alternate with other foot (note spontaneous choice of feet).
• Balance on tip toe. Same movements as above but on tip toe.

Equilibrium in Motion

Note the patient's understanding, co-ordination and quality of performance.
• Walking: ask the patient to walk about in the room (for very inhibited subjects, give an aim, eg. 'Go and open the door please'.
• Running: verbal request, no gestures.
• Jumping: on one foot, on the other foot, and hop on alternate feet.

Co-ordination

The following exercises are to evaluate the ability to contract various muscle groups independently from others; also to evaluate the knowledge of the various parts of the face.

Co-ordination of the face. (Kwint Test, R. Zazzo)

Bilateral movements of the face: frowning, showing teeth etc. and unilateral movements of the face: shut one eye, whistle etc.

General Co-ordination: Rapid alternative movements (note individual limb movements).

Puppet test – forearms bent vertically, hands at chin level;

rotate wrists to bring hands alternatively in pronation and supination.

Association Movements of Limbs

● Upper limbs: touch left shoulder with left hand, the other arm is stretched laterally; inverse movement several times.

● Upper limbs/head: same activities (but hand touches the head) plus a rotation of the head towards the outstretched arm.

● Upper limbs/lower limbs: same activities as above plus elevation of knee on the same side as outstretched arm.

● Upper limbs/lower limbs/head: combination of all previous activities.

Finger Dexterity

Assessment of fine motor discrimination and independence of each finger.

● Opposition of thumb with other fingers (starting from index to little finger and vice versa).

● Stretching fingers apart (two thumbs first).

● Flexing of fingers (hands held up at shoulder level).

● Drumming of fingers on the table.

Syncinesiae

Patient stands up, feet together, facing the therapist.

1. Fine movements of fingers (syncinesiae – observed during the previous tests).

2. Puppet movement – to be performed with one hand (same position as previously) opposite arm alongside the body. Same exercises with the other hand.

● Same movement with both arms alongside the body: one and then the other hand.

● Same movement arms stretched out horizontally and forwards.

These three tests can be performed eyes closed.

3. Foot/hand syncinesiae: feet together, tips of feet apart, keep the heels together.

4. Mouth/hands: alternative opening and shutting of lips, mouth (wide open).

Note: The localisation of the syncinesiae – contro-lateral, bi- or unilateral (in Test 3 and 4) axial.

5. Form of syncinesiae – syncinesiae of imitation (reproduction of opposite hand movements).

6. Intensity of syncinesiae (light, average or marked tonical diffusion).

7. Direction of syncinesiae: note that the dominant hand syncinesiae are less marked.

Laterality

Hand

• Praxis: ask the patient to perform various daily and spontaneous movements such as: combing one's hair, brushing one's teeth, etc.

• Dotting (stippling) Test. A sheet of paper divided in two (left/right) is given to the patient who holds a pencil in each hand. Ask him to draw with both hands at the same time a series of repetitive dots on the same spot.

• Same test standing up.

The side where the dots are closer together is the dominant side.

• Observations noticed in other tests are taken into consideration, eg. finger dexterity, graphism, drawing direction of syncinesiae, degree of relaxation.

Eyes

• Aiming: Looking through a rolled up sheet of paper.

• Sighting: Looking through a hole in a piece of paper held first at arm's length, then progressively closer until it is close to the dominant eye.

• Check which eye has been chosen.

Feet

Note the choice of dominant feet when:

• Standing on one foot.

• Kicking a ball or pushing an object with the foot.

Tonus and Relaxation

Appreciation of Passiveness globally and separately for each part of limbs (hands, forearms, etc).

• Dangling movement of upper limbs. Check the degree of relaxation of manipulating the shoulder so as to induce large oscillations of the arms. Appreciate the dangling movement of the whole arms, of the forearms and hands.

• Drop arm from horizontal each in turn.

• Passive flexion of forearm several times: slowly, rapidly, with a sudden stop. Check the same elements as above; in the case of rapid mobilisation with a sudden stop, check if there is continuation of the movement.

Ability to Relax: Such exercises are often not carried out during the first assessment as many patients cannot cope with them and become very worried and tense. These reactions make it impossible to assess the ability of the patient to relax – therefore, they are often carried out once a sound relationship has been established between patient and therapist.

The patient position is dorsal decubitus (lying down on back on a mat), the head can be supported by a cushion, hands and legs are slightly abducted (hands in pronation). Request: 'Relax as much as possible, try to be all soft and floppy, like a puppet or a rag doll.' Test the state of relaxation by swinging a limb, then dropping it suddenly. Upper and lower limbs are assessed.

In case of paratonia: try to appreciate the form of paratonia with 'Paratonia of action': the subject cannot intentionally stop it. This is part of the symptoms encountered with motor debility. Paratonia can be caused by the emotional state facing a testing situation. Such manifestations are obviously not linked with the motor state but indicate the subject's fragility when relating to others or when under stress.

Extensibility: The relaxation of limbs is evaluated by the manipulation of the limbs and the stretching of a few muscles. In the upper limbs, with patient standing, assess the elbow joints (stretching bracchial biceps, bending of forearms) and the shoulder joints (stretching of deltoid muscle). In the lower limbs assess the knee joint (stretching of quadriceps), the flexion of the leg or thigh and foot joint (stretching of the back flexor and abductor muscles). In each test check the degree of extension given by the opening of the angle of the joints which varies with the typologies – Asthenic types are usually hyperlaxed; athletic types are less supple. Also check the variation of extensibility between each side. There is often a physiological variation limited with the dominance (right hand less extensible if dominant) which is less marked in young children.

Writing and Graphism

Spontaneous graphism – The patient is asked to write his name and a sentence of his choice. If he refuses to write anything down, try to dictate a sentence. Check the choice of

hand, the ease, rapidity and quality of graphism. This test may also give information on the level of organisation of written language and in the spelling. The content of the sentence may also be of some help.

Graphism: Such tests are only used with children presenting laterality problems or poor writing.

Ask them to draw wavy or mountain-like lines, curls, etc. (See Hand/Eye Co-ordination). Check the quality of the drawing; suppleness and continuity of movement; whether hand, arm and shoulders are relaxed while writing; and syncinesiae. Refer to tests of motor maturation and of laterality to fully evaluate the results.

Temporo-Spatial Organisation

Drawing without copying: a house, and a person. Later on in therapy, it will be interesting to ask him to draw a picture of the subject's family. Also comments on the quality of the drawing.

Drawing with copy: Ask the patient to copy the drawings on page 89. Check the quality of the reproduction, the organisation of the various elements of the bicycle and compare the drawings from copy and from memory. The Bender Test and the Khos Cubes are often used in association with the above tests.

Rhythm: Reproduction of 21 rhythmic structures from the Mira-Stamback Test (structures are clapped) eg: 1. 000, 9. 00 000, 21.0 00 00 0 00. Check the number of the structures achieved successfully at the first attempt and at the second attempt.

Orientation: Left and right concepts, body knowledge from head's left and right orientation test. For example execute the following demands: Facing the therapist – right hand on right eye, left hand on left ear, etc. The same exercises are then transposed on to the therapist ('Place my right hand on my left shoulder', etc). For reversibility do the same as therapist, who corrects patient if gestures are reroduced in 'mirror'.

Imitation of meaningless gestures performed by therapist. (J. Berges and I. Lezine Test). These are arm gestures, hand gestures, and hand and finger gestures.

This psychomotor assessment has been developed by H. Bucher. Various similar psychomotor assessments have been elaborated by G. Soubiran, M. Vyl, Picq and Vayer etc. This later assessment presents the advantage of assessing the psychomotor development according to an age chart. Results are expressed visually on a chart showing weaknesses in psychomotor development and therapeutic needs (*see below*).

Example of Psychomotor Graphic Profile (L. Picq and P. Vayer)

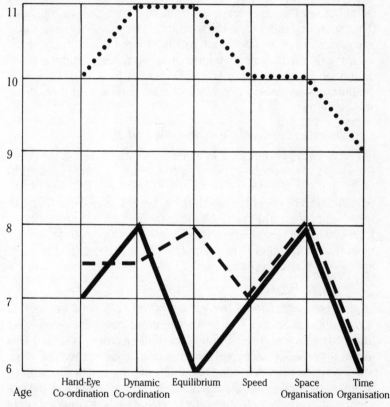

Patient – Paul L. (8 years old at the time of first assessment)
I.Q.: 0.75 (Terman Test)
Problems: school delay, affective and behavioural difficulties

━━━ 1st assessment
━ ━ 2nd assessment
•••• 3rd assessment

Psychomotor Techniques and Media

Therapeutic methods concern the re-education of specific psychomotor disorders (body image, space, etc) and the approach of the psychological difficulties and of the problems the patient experiences when relating to others. Therapeutic activities and media vary a lot from one therapist to the next. This section describes a few specific activities and therapeutic methods, but it is important to underline that each therapist adapts and creates his own kind of approaches within the main frame of psychomotor therapeutic techniques. The following techniques are used in combination according to the needs of the patient:

Specific Psychomotor Activities

Specific psychomotor activities are established in line with the stages of psychomotor development, the age and personality of the patient, the degree of his handicap, etc. They aim at the re-education of specific disorders eg. body image. However it is important to remind the reader that the groups of exercises are inter-related. The activities listed below are only guidelines or prototypes on which the therapist bases his design for each specific remedial programme.

BODY IMAGE

First Stage: Global perception of the body, of its unity and its position in space. This first stage concerns the awareness of the body as a whole, as a unity and of its position in space. This allows the person to experience his body as a whole. The more disorganised the body image is, the more important this step is. Unless the child has experienced certain elements of permanence of his body, activities only referring to the manipulation of the limbs for instance could not be taken in and could even convey a sensation of uneasiness and incompleteness. So it is very important to rebuild the unity of the body prior to starting any analytic activities. The aim is to enable the subject to experience his body, its various postures and the impressions created by his moving in space. The activities will include:

- The different positions of the body in space: standing, sitting, lying down, kneeling down. The patient must acquire a clear picture of such positions. They must be referred to with precise words and explained if necessary.
- The various forms of movement using the whole of the body: walking (various forms), jumping, running, rolling, crawling (the different points of contact on the ground are important as well as stopping, keeping still, etc).

Various aspects and concepts are added to these activities for instance with walking the variations apply to:

- the quality of the walk: slowly, big steps, etc.
- the changing of rhythm using a tambourine
- the changing of directions to the right/left etc.
- the use of space when walking (on a line, freely, etc.)
- the use of feet: walk on toes, heels etc.

Integration and improvement are achieved by the use of contrasts throughout and of more and more subtle variations leading to a finer discrimination. A child experiences these forms of movement in any spontaneous activity or play, but they often are not differentiated, are confused, and have no bearing with the verbal designation. The psychomotor therapist by means of appropriate movements, and verbalisation, changes the patient's confused activity into an awareness of his position in space and the mastering of his body.

Second stage first spatial data: The patient must have assimilated the previous data before he can move to the second stage. The experiences here are carried out with reference to the previous global positions (walk, run, etc). The patient learns to differentiate the various positions of each limb separately and in relation to the rest of his body. This relies on a motor experience involving proprioceptive and exteroceptive elements. This stage concerns:

- the learning of data relative to the immediate space: eg. in front of me, behind me, above, below, beside, etc.
- the main parts of the body: joints, different parts of limbs, etc.
- the various positions of the different parts of the limbs, alongside the body, stretched out, etc.
- the precise concepts of simple bodily positions and attitudes.
  The learning of such positions and attitudes is done
- with guidance and corrections facing a mirror

- without guidance facing a mirror
- without guidance and without a mirror
- without guidance eyes shut.

Awareness of body gestural space. Figures 1–3 show the patient standing up, learning to find the accurate horizontal and vertical positions of the arms. Figures 4–7 show the patient finding the accurate position of the arms and forearms in relation to specific parts of the body. Similarly with the various positions of the lower limbs such as feet together, one foot in front of the other, one leg stretched the other bent, etc. The same activities are carried out with spatial concepts eg. in front of, behind, etc.

Knowledge of the body. Learning to localise and name the different parts of the body: limbs, trunk, head, face, joints, feet and hands by:
- physical contact; therapist touches knee, elbow, etc, and patient has to name these. This enables the patient to experience a sensation concerning the part of the body that is being touched.
- obeying requests such as 'put your hands on your eyes, on your forehead, on your hips', etc and 'put your hands in front of your face, on either side of your head', etc (introduction of spatial data).
- the use of the body as a reference point, a pivot.

Such activities will come last when a sufficient knowledge of the previous concepts has been acquired: awareness of the body as a whole, knowledge and perceptions of the various positions of limbs relative to the immediate space. Finally the concept of right and left ('put your left hand on your left knee') is then introduced. The position in the room must vary to prevent using the walls or an item of furniture as a reference point.

LATERALITY

The aim of the psychomotor therapist will be to help the patient become familiar with the concept of left and right, so as to improve his body awareness and control, his spatial recognition, and writing and reading difficulties. This will be conveyed once again through experiencing the body in action. Through movement, and through doing, the concepts of right and left become part of the individual. The activities advocated for general laterality difficulties are usually those for body image, spatial organisation, hand-eye and general co-ordination. In the case of constitutional lefthandedness the therapist usually aims at re-creating correct motor habits for learning reading and writing.

SPATIAL ORGANISATION

Concepts of right, left, behind, etc. can only be integrated through personal experience, when the individual is moving and has to position his body in space according to external demands. Activities concerning spatial structure follow a careful progression. They first deal with the individual's immediate space, then concern his transposition of that space to others and in relation to objects.

Immediate space: appreciation of the various directions and orientation in space. Concepts of right, left, in front of, behind.

• awareness of those concepts on the body (eg. in front is my tummy, behind is my back, etc).

• awareness of the same concepts in motion eg. standing in a hoop and on request step to the right, left, etc. The position of patient and hoops is changed to enable the patient to become aware of the constance of his personal marks (eg. to use his body as a reference point).

These are followed by the introduction of new spatial

concepts such as: above, below, in the middle, etc. and the introduction of various other forms of movement such as: jump to the right and hop to the left with variation on the size of the movement (eg. one giant step to the right, two dwarf steps to the left, etc.) Ball throwing is used eg. to the left, right, etc. on demand, and the appreciation of the horizontal and vertical positions of the body and the constance of the various directions in these positions.

Orientation in relation to external objects. Learning to position oneself: in relation to one object, eg. in front of a chair, behind it, etc. and in relation to two objects, eg. on the left of the chair and on the right of the bench. The position of the objects in the room are changed, and the same activities are repeated.

Transposition to other persons. When the various directions are well integrated a partner (the therapist or another patient) joins in. The patient has to learn to keep his own marks without letting himself be influenced by the actions of his partner and to reproduce the movement and actions of his partner. Suggested games are:-

• The Sculptor: (patient plus two partners) one partner is used as a model, the other is the 'statue'. The patient is the sculptor who has reproduced the various positions of his model on the statue; (then roles are changed).

• Use of a set route. Various objects are scattered around the room on the floor. The therapist walks a particular route and the patient has to remember and walk the same route. This can be reproduced on paper. (This involves mental representation.)

• Objects are scattered on the floor, the patient has to guide the therapist (or partner) using only verbal instructions so that he knocks these objects over, eg. take two steps forward, then three to the left.

Activities with distances and intervals aid the development of concepts such as close, far, short, long; close together, far apart, etc. They also teach the appreciation of the distance between various objects or between personal position and an outside element. This is achieved when the movement intended reaches its purpose (eg. throwing a ball in a basket). Here games are also linked with hand-eye co-ordination and dynamic co-ordination. Kinaesthesic sensations are used to support and correct visual appreciation of distance. Suggested games are the adaptation of movement to distances:

• Jumping or skipping etc. into hoops arranged at various distances and intervals, eg. at regular intervals: 0 0 0 0 then at irregular intervals: 00 0 0 000

• Throwing a ball with precision into hoops on the floor (left, right, forwards, etc.); throwing a ball over obstacles from various distances and throwing into a basket.

• Same activities while in motion. For instance throwing a ball into a basket while running and avoiding obstacles (chairs, benches, etc.) at the same time.

Perception of the third dimension: appreciation of the trajectory. Activities here are similar to those for dynamic co-ordination. Ball games are often used and are planned as a function of the therapeutic aim – games such as pig in the middle, and catching and throwing balls from various distances with one or several partners can be used. Vary the size and numbers of balls to convey different experiences.

Relationship between space and time.

• Appreciation of speed in personal action: slow or fast walk (how much ground is covered in a set amount of time), slow and fast race and rolling a ball slowly, quickly, etc.

• Appreciation of personal speed compared with the speed of a partner: running together first at the same speed, then at different speeds.

• Appreciation of one's personal speed compared with the speed of a moving object: run faster, slower, at the same speed as the ball, etc.

• Comparison of the speed of different objects, e.g. throwing two balls to a partner at different/same speeds, and throwing one ball first then the other so that it can catch up with the first one.

Mental representation of spatial concepts – Work at the desk. (left, right, above, etc.) Dictation of verbal directions to be reproduced on a piece of squared paper in order to obtain a recognisable pattern (see diagrams, page 98). For instance: two squares to the left, one up, etc. Khos cubes are often used at the final stages to reinforce the spatial data the patient has acquired. Khos cubes are testing equipment consisting of a set of sixteen cubes and number of patterned cards. Each side of the cube shows a different pattern. The patterns outlined on the cards have to be reproduced by use of the cubes.

Other techniques. Artistic elements and music can be associated once elementary concepts have been assimilted and once the patient has learnt to cope with other partners. Then activities such as country dancing which require good co-ordination, good concentration, good organisation of space and time (appreciation of speed, distances, rhythm, etc) can be helpful activities. Such creative social involvement fosters, maintains, and makes use of the acquired psychomotor skills.

Mental representation of space notions: a few examples:-

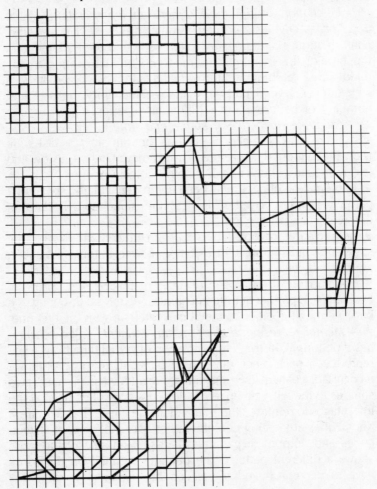

TIME ORGANISATION
Acquisition of basic elements

• Concept of speed. Adaptation to a given rhythm: eg. walk at various speeds dictated by a metronome. Other movements such as swinging arms reinforce the feeling of rapidity, of slowness, etc. It is advised to start with slow and easy rhythms similar to the personal spontaneous tempo, then to increase the speed and to ask patients to describe them verbally. Elements from 'co-ordination' or 'space' can be borrowed to strengthen the effect of these rhythmical experiences.

• Concept of duration. Two examples are firstly covering a certain distance walking, then running, then verbalization of feelings, which was quicker or slower, etc. and secondly the therapist plays a sound with variation in length – the patient transcripts it on a board: ———— Long ——Short.

• Continuity and reversibility. These concepts are described above.

• Concept of interval. (See paragraph on rhythm)

Awareness of time relationships. The aim is to develop the awareness of:

• Simultaneity and succession: Repeat simultaneously walking and clapping a rhythm.

• The 'present time', the moment when something happens/the precise moment. The therapist walks from point A in a room to point B. The patient is asked to clap his hands just as the therapist passes in front of him. Same thing with balls rolling on the floor, and clapping hands at the precise moment when they pass in front of patient, etc. Throwing ball and clapping hands when it touches the ground, etc.

• 'Before' and 'After'. Walking from point A to point B – and clapping hands before passing in front of the therapist and after; and the same with balls. This can be represented graphically:

$$\text{Therapist}$$
$$A \underline{\hspace{3cm}} X \underline{\hspace{3cm}} B \longrightarrow$$
$$\text{clap} \qquad\qquad \text{clap}$$

• Awareness of succession. This also concerns spatial concepts – rhythms are represented by the position of various objects in space eg. balls are placed as follows on the floor:

O O o o O O

Take one step between each ball and beat the rhythm on a tambourine at the same time. In this case two loud beats, two soft beats, two loud beats.

Co-ordination of all elements. Combinations of various rhythms involving speed, duration, intervals, simultaneity, etc; for example repeating the previous activity at different speeds.

Slow O O o o O O
Fast OOoOO
and so on.

RHYTHM

The first task of the therapist when designing rhythmic activities is to listen to the natural 'tempo' or natural rhythm of his patient. Some patients will get completely inhibited if asked to reproduce a slow rhythm while others will find it easier. For this reason three different speeds of rhythm can be selected: slow, intermediate, fast. Rhythm underlines the difficulty the patient has in controlling his movement and the quality of his ability to concentrate. Rhythm can improve such weaknesses.

The acquisition of concepts of rhythm (regular, irregular) and of pace (slower and quicker) can include listening to the tambourine and

• saying whether it is a regular rhythm ('always the same') or irregular.
• clapping to the rhythm and saying whether it is slower or faster in comparison to the given rhythm.
• walking or stamping these rhythms.
• same as above with accentuation on one clap or stamp.

Also graphic reproducton eg:

o o o o o o o o o o o   regular quick rhythm
o   o   o   o   o   regular slow rhythm

o oo   o   ooo oo   o   irregular rhythm

o O o O o O o O o O o   regular rhythm with accentuation on one clap

Later the introduction of more complex rhythms with clapping and walking simultaneously to a rhythm or walk 3 beats, clap the 3 following beats ... and so on up to various degrees of complexity. Finally the adaptation to a partner. The patient then has to develop more concentration and not be influenced by his partner's action.

CO-ORDINATION

Such activities aim at giving more accuracy to the movement and more control over it.

Improvement of Automatic Patterns

• Walking and Running. The aims during such movements are to create an awareness and education of sensations (contact points with the ground, walk on heel, tip toes, etc.), to eliminate superfluous movements (eg. swinging arms, twisting head), to develop uprightness of trunk, postural control and balance mechanisms and adapt these to space and time eg. size of the steps, walking between bricks and walking or running carrying bean bags on the head.

• Climbing, on apparatus, off apparatus, climbing higher, climbing in relation to space (up to a set height).

• Jumping. Activities on the ground in relation to space (jump on the spot, to the right, left, following various patterns), in connection with rhythm, in connection with obstacles of varying heights and the control of the impulse (over a line, a rope, a book, etc.), running or standing jumps, varying forms of jumps (feet together, hopping, etc.) and jumping from various heights (in progression: jumps from bricks, benches, chairs, beams, etc. in connection with previous variations relative to space, rhythm, forms of jumps, etc.).

Relevant balance and postural activities are included – see paragraph on Balance.

Skilful and collective games. These are usually greatly enjoyed by children because they involve playing. Sometimes they can be the only way to approach negative or immature subjects. Their adaptability and variety offers the advantage of the possibility of working either individually or in a group.

• Ball games. It is important to vary the size, weight and texture of balls and to adapt activities to the needs of the patient to provide varied experiences. It is important to plan a carefully set progression. Equipment and work become more complex as therapy goes on, varying in time, space and movement factors. Eventually, they will lead to collective ball or skill games, eg. familiarisation with objects (manipulation of balls, education of the grips); throwing and catching (with one hand, two hands, from various directions and heights, between obstacles, on a wall, in association with other movements such as clapping, stamping, etc.); adaptation to space and movement (dribbling movements associated with walking, running, etc. introducing various rhythms, speeds and directions, throwing from various heights); introduce concept of precision (throwing a ball in a basket, varying the position of the basket); adaptation to a partner (repeat with one partner, then with a small group); co-ordination of a number of movements (two commands are given at the same time eg. dribbling while walking round the room and carrying out the therapist's verbal requests relative to directions, speeds, etc.); throwing and catching two balls at the same time (one with the left hand, the other one with the right hand).

• Games with Hoops. Learning to stop on signal (hoops are placed in a circle. The patient runs around them; on a signal he has to jump in one of the hoops. Repeat this game several times), leading to more complex demands (When the tambourine is played, stand in the red hoop. When the bell is played, stand on one foot in the blue hoop. If a whistle is played, sit in the green hoop, and so on.).

• Games with Skipping Ropes. These are based on the principles previously outlined and follow a similar progression. Such activities involve the control of the impulse, the adaptation to exterior elements such as speed, rhythms, direction, etc.

• Movement dissociation concerning both upper and lower limbs. Performing more and more complex movements in co-ordination with variations in rhythm, orientation in space, etc.

The games the therapist can propose are numerous. Hélène Buchet describes many of them in her book *The Psychomotor Disorders of the Child*.

HAND-EYE CO-ORDINATION

Without good hand-eye co-ordination a person cannot achieve skills such as reading and writing. Poor hand-eye co-ordination leads to imprecision of movement. For re-education of hand-eye co-ordination much of the previous therapy is indicated, in combination with time and space activities. Suggested activities include:

• Throwing and catching balls, stressing the importance of following the ball with the eyes, keeping eye contact with it, and the necessity of fine motor dexterity.

• Space and time experiences concerning the appreciation of distances, relations in space and appreciation of concepts such as duration, speed, simultaneity, etc.

• Grapho-motor exercises or pre-writing exercises: the patient has to draw simple forms at first, then more complex ones. He is first requested to walk them, then to reproduce them on a board, then on paper. Examples of pre-writing exercises (*see below*).

• Other suggestions of work at a desk only eg. putting tails on mice, hair on heads, smiles on faces, etc.

EQUILIBRIUM AND POSTURAL CONTROL

Many activities used for dynamic co-ordination serve the double purpose of also improving dynamic balance mechanisms (activities described previously involving walking, running, skipping and jumping – see page 101). It is important to build up the patient's confidence by a slow and careful progression: this progression also concerns how to fall (for activities on beam for instance), getting accustomed to heights, and the gradual withdrawal of the therapist's help.

Balance activities, contact or proximity to the ground. Preparation: Stand on one foot and maintain the position, holding on to gym bars, left knee up; stretch it to the right, left, backwards, etc. The use of the bar is gradually withdrawn. Repeat on bench and on wooden bricks. Practise in varied positions. The aim is to maintain the posture with various positions of the arms eg. on one foot: bend forwards, backwards. Various games can be made out of these activities (pushing a brick with the foot). Continue into squatting position then walk in these positions. Finally progress to hops and skips and jumps on one leg pushing one cube between various objects with the other foot without losing balance, etc.

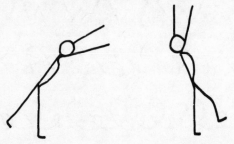

Balance on beam. Grade therapist's help from holding on to therapist's hand throughout the activities; then give it up gradually, only using it if necessary; to finally no aid given. The therapist must be vigilant, ready to help if necessary. Develop the activity as follows:- stand on beam, walk on beam, walk on beam with various arm gestures, walk on beam and lift one leg on signal, walk on tiptoe, walk on tiptoe with a beanbag on head, kneel down on beam, kneel down and pick up an object on beam, walk backwards, sideways, and catch a ball and throw it back, vary the trajectories, etc.

Balance on unstable objects eg. medicine balls, weighted balls, sandbags. Stand on ball and vary positions on ball. Catch and throw a ball using various trajectories and cross a 'ford' made of weighted balls or sandbags without touching the ground (vary the distances between the bags, vary the number of bags).

Eyes shut – Balance Control. Suitable activities can be repeated without visual guidance. (Only suitable if the patient is confident and skilful enough.)

Relaxation Therapy

Relaxation therapy holds an important place in psychomotor therapy. It is a technique that improves the general control of movement and the accuracy of intentional gestures by bringing ease to the body and suppressing parasitic muscular tensions. Such physical ease helps the patient to 'unwind' and induces a feeling of mental relaxation.

Relaxation therapy also contributes to the elaboration of body image by enabling various tonic states to be experienced.

This therapy is particularly prescribed for paratonia, motor-debility and emotional and tonical disorders such as tics, certain forms of stammering, clumsiness, hyperactivity, etc. It must be used carefully according to the age, emotional state and intellectual ability of the subject.

With young children (under 9) muscular relaxation is usually rapidly obtained. However, further stages of relaxation are difficult to attain. The child is passive, lacks initiative and relies upon the therapist's intervention. As the child grows older he can learn to inhibit his muscular tonus in the same way that he learns to adjust his postures and movements through various exercises. With older children the degree of subjectivity increases. The link between the tonical and the affective states (emotion, inhibition, anxiety, conflict at home, at school, etc.) is more pronounced.

With disturbed persons, particularly those presenting body image delay, relaxation therapy cannot be approached directly. The same problem arises with mentally handicapped patients; their understanding is limited and therefore their approach to relaxation must be kept very simple. With such persons, and also because it is easier and less stressful, relaxation therapy should take place at the end of an active session, and aims at conveying a certain calm and quietness to the patient.

Here again as at any other level in pscyhomotor therapy methods should not be too set or rigid. The diversity of the exercises enables the therapist to adapt his work to the patient's needs as opportunities arise. The technique of relaxation taught then progresses to be an experience of the whole body. The accent can be set on either side of the relaxation aims
• the acquisition and mastery of an economic and adequate tonus
• the experiencing of self awareness and the discovery of the body as a whole.

The following method has been developed from the Schultz method by H. Bucher. Other similar methods such as the Soubiran and Jacobson Methods are available.

PREPARATORY WORK

It takes time for the therapist to build up a trusting relationship with his patient. Most patients are at first uneasy and tense, and present defence mechanisms and various ways of reacting to the situation. The therapist himself does not know his patient; they both need time to get to know, trust and adapt to each other before they can work in tune.

The easiest way to introduce relaxation therapy is to bring it in at the end of active games and activities that provoke fatigue or breathlessness as this naturally leads to calmer activities and to a period of recuperation, rest and quietness. This period is not always well accepted by patients. However, a restful state can be progressively attained more spontaneously and more intensely. Often after a few sessions the patient himself chooses to go and lie down for a rest.

During relaxation therapy the therapist takes the opportunity to make the person aware of certain sensations: breathlessness, respiratory and cardiac rhythms, warmth, heaviness. Progressively this rest period becomes an exercise as such, to which the patient may look forward. It leads towards more specific and complex activities in connection with the awareness and knowledge of one's body and feelings.

Relaxation therapy can be practised in various positions. The patient can sit, stand or lie down, according to the needs and stages of the therapy.

PARTIAL RELAXATION

Preliminary. Partial relaxation turns the patient's attention to one particular part of their body; helps the release of uneasiness at a stage where most could not tolerate a general relaxation. Later on in the therapy relaxation will be generalised. With verbal explanation ensure that the subject understands what is required. The vocabulary used must be simple and familiar to the patient, particularly for a child. For instance for 'contract and relax' use instead picturesque comparisons eg. 'now your arm is floppy, soft, imagine you are a rag doll'. Or on the contrary: 'now you are a stiff piece of wood: keep your arm as hard and as stiff as a tree trunk'. The patient can check the degree of contraction by touching and manipulating the therapist's arm or leg and feeling the degree of contraction.

The awareness and acquisition of tonical control is obtained through:

- personal action with contrast activities (relax/contract)
- the therapist checks the patient's body to ascertain the degree of relaxation
- awareness of localised and precise sensations
- verbal analysis of sensations and modification of the tonical state
- the end of the exercise is marked by an 'awakening', according to the Schultz method: forearm flexion, deep breathing exercises, and eventually opening the eyes.

Relaxation for the Upper Limbs

These exercises are first executed with one arm (right if right handed patient, etc.) then with the other, then both arms.

- Personal Action: Contrast exercises in 2 possible positions:-
The patient lies on his back, arms away from his body, hands in pronation, legs slightly abducted and toes toward the outside. His head can rest on a cushion.
The patient lies on his front, head to one side, arms alongside his body. Requests such as: lift up then drop; stretch out then relax; bend then relax, press on mat then relax concern the hand, forearm and arm, wrist (elbow and finger tips remain in contact with the mat), shoulder, the whole limb in various directions.

- Passivity: With the patient lying on his back, check the degree of relaxation for: hand, wrist, fingers, whole arm, forearm, arm, shoulder. For each manipulation check the ease of the drop, the ease of movement in the joints, the degree of relaxation, the degree of participation (or passivity). Repeat with patient lying on his front.

• Study of sensations. Perception of support and contact points with the floor and study of the sensation of heaviness for the various parts of the upper limbs.

• Verbalised study of sensations and of various modifications of the tonical state. Such verbalisation helps the patient to recognise and locate the sensations. It contributes to the progression of the subject through his discoveries and analyses, by exchanging and confronting views with the therapist. At this stage the patient takes an active part in the therapy.

Relaxation Exercises for the Lower Limbs. Exercises are similar to those for the upper limbs: personal action, passivity and so on, foot, leg, knee, thigh, whole limb, etc.

Exercises for both Lower and Upper Limbs. As above, same fourfold method ie. contrast activities, study of sensation, verbal analysis. This is done in symmetry (right upper and lower limb, left upper and lower limb), in asymmetry, in alternance and simultaneously.

Exercises for the Relaxation of the Trunk. Same methods when possible. Concerns shoulders, hips, abdomen, patient lying on his back, front and sitting.

Exercises for the Relaxation of Face, Nape and Neck. These areas of our bodies can reflect more specifically psychological tensions and emotions and must only be approached when the subject is able to reach a certain degree of relaxation in other parts of the body. The same exercises and methods as previously described are used ie. contrast exercises eg: lift head, let it drop; close eyes tightly, relax; etc.

Awareness of Respiration. The patient has been made aware of his breathing during the preparatory work. He is now required to execute a few exercises to analyse functions and sensations that are normally automatic. These exercises also enable many patients to improve the quality of their breathing.

• Breathing out, observing intensity, length, holding of the breath and associated sensations. First breathing out through mouth then nostrils.

• Breathing in as above but breathing in only through nostrils.

• Study rib movements.

- Study abdominal movements.

Association of Relaxation and Respiration Exercises. Combine the previous exercises to link the contraction (clenching, lifting, etc.) to the breathing in and relaxation to breathing out.

GENERAL RELAXATION

Personal action: contrast activities. Patient lying on his back, complete stretching out of the body, trunk, limbs, etc. Relax. Curl the whole body up knee to chin, arms folded round legs. Relax and unwind the body. Similar activities in frontal position.

Passivity. Passive mobilisation of the various parts of the whole body. Check the quality of relaxation and breathing.

Study of sensation with verbalisation. In connection with relaxation, experience warmth, tingling feelings, heaviness, spreading out, swelling, etc. In connection with breathing, experience gentle rocking or swaying sensations; the patient may feel as if his body is moving in space. In connection with mental relaxation, experience drowsiness, mental emptiness and slowing down, sensation of facial relaxation (particularly eyes and forehead), sensation of well being, easiness, recovery, readiness for action.

It is important to make sure that the physiological reactions described above are well supported by the therapist as they can induce anxiety and fear; particularly those sensations linked to the variations of body image and deplacement in space. The role of the therapist through verbalisation is to enable his patient to understand, rationalise such changes, to reassure him, enabling him to go a step further in the relaxation exercises. If such a reassurance cannot be achieved and the anxiety and fears persist, then the exercise should be cut short or stopped altogether.

SUGGESTIONS OF MENTAL THEMES OR IMAGES

When the patient has learnt to relax, various mental pictures or themes can be suggested to him (eg. you are outside lying down in a meadow – what can you see, hear, etc?).

Hydrotherapy

The aquatic environment offers further opportunities to work with and express one's body.

Immersed in water, our body can experience different sensations relative to gravity, temperature and water pressure. It has to adapt to such changes and can explore new possibilities. In the water a different way of moving can be experienced; a way of moving with reduced gravity. This is very helpful to the physically handicapped patient who will be able to experience the pleasure of a certain ease and freedom of movement. Water can therefore help with some specific re-educative activities (eg. finding the right posture in order to obtain a better balance control).

The aquatic environment was first experienced in intra-uterine life and this may be the reason why so many disturbed patients such as psychotic and autistic patients react positively to it. Not only does water bring pleasure to them, encouraging their relaxation, it also stimulates their interest and senses, their awareness of their surroundings and of the therapist working with them. It encourages them to move about and learn about their own bodies. For instance they may discover their respiration by breathing water in and will have to control it in order to avoid doing this. They have to adapt respiration, movement, etc, to the water element. It allows them to release pent up energy through movement; most people experience a sensation of relaxation after a session in the pool.

Various ball games and activities take on another dimension in water and can aid development of certain motor skills (eg. adaptation to the different gravity).

Corporal Expression – Role Play

Corporal expression is used by psychomotor therapists to encourage the patient to express his feelings more freely and to overcome his inhibitions. Through this form of therapy the patient learns to control his defence mechanisms and to gain confidence in himself. This technique can be used individually or in a group according to the requirement of the remedial programme and to the needs and ability of the patients. During the corporal expression session the patient is asked (sometimes shown first) to express his feelings in movements. Various themes and medias are proposed: musical themes, drama (sketches can be performed with alternating roles, masks can be worn), mime, etc.

The Use of Music

Music is often used with various psychomotor activities:
- with certain re-educative activities to make them more attractive, to introduce auditory stimulus
- with rhythm to test and improve the patient's ability to adapt and recognise various rhythms
- with corporal expression
- to improve auditory discrimination (nature of instruments, contrast between noise and silence)
- to express various moods (happiness, sadness, anger, peace)
- to relax a hyperactive child (often in association with relaxation therapy) or to stimulate an apathetic one (particularly in the case of children or adolescents with psychotic tendencies).

The Training of the Psycho-Re-Educator

In France psycho-re-educators are state qualified, attaining a State Diploma after the completion of a three-year course. They are controlled by the Ministry of Health.

Admission Conditions: Candidates have to be in possession of the Baccalaureat and an attestation given by the DRASS (Direction Regionale de L'Action Sanitaire et Sociale).

Studies: Curriculum and Practical Studies:

● First Year Examination:- General initiation, General and Neuro-anatomy, Physiology, Psychology, Pedagogy, Pedopsychiatry, Psychomotricity, meetings, discussions, etc. At the end of the first year, an Examination is held to limit the number of places in accordance with the national needs determined by the Health Ministry.

● Second Year: Functional Anatomy, Physiology and Physiopathology, Pediatry, Psychology, Child Psychiatry, Psychomotricity.

● Third Year: Psychology, Psychiatry, Psychomotricity, Legislation and Deontology.

Each year, particularly the third year, includes personal training, case studies and probation time spent in creches, nurseries, psychiatric hospitals and special schools.

Examination and State Degrees. Examinations are held at the end of each academic year and involve theoretical and practical tests. The student must also present a thesis.

Bibliography

Ajuriaguerra, J de, *Manuel de psychiatrie de l'enfant*, Masson et Cie

Bergés, J et Lézine, I., *Test d'imitation de gestes*, Masson et Cie

Bossu, H. et Chalaguier, C., *L'expression corporelle*, Le Centurion

Bucher, H., *Troubles psychomoteurs chez l'enfant*, Masson et Cie

Guilhmain, *Tests moteurs et psychomoteurs*, Foyer Central d'Hygiene

Herren, H. and M.P., *La stimulation psychomotrice du nourrisson*, Masson et Cie

Le Camus, J., *Pratiques psychomotrices*, Psychologie et Sciences Humaines

Piaget, J. et Inhelder, *La représentation de l'espace chez l'enfant*, P.U.F.

Piaget, J., *Le développement de la notion de temps chez l'enfant*, P.U.F.

Piaget, J., *Motricité, perception, intelligence*, Enfance

Picq, L. et Vayer, P., *Education psycho-motrice et arriération mentale*, Doin

Soubiran et Coste, *Psychomotricité et relaxation psychosomatique*, Doin

Wallon, H., *De l'acte à la pensée*, Flammarion

Wallon, H., *Les origines du caractère chez l'enfant*, P.U.F.

Zazzo, *Manuel pour l'examen psychologique de l'enfant*, Delachaux et Nestlé

Addresses

Institut Supérieur de Ré-éducation Psychomotrice
9 rue de Bouquet de Longchamp 75116 Paris

Université Paris VI, U.E.R. de Medecine Pitié-Salpêtrière
47 Boulevard de l'Hôpital, 75006 Paris
Section Psychomotricité

CHAPTER 3

MOVEMENT THROUGH MUSIC

By Priscilla Barclay

> *"Would it not be possible to create new reflexes; undertake the education of the nervous centres; to calm over active temperaments; to order antagonisms; to harmonise energies; to establish more direct communication between the mind and the senses?"*
>
> **EMILE JAQUES-DALCROZE**

History

In the early years of this century Emile Jaques-Dalcroze, professor at the Conservatoire of Music in Geneva, asked himself these questions. He was concerned with the lack of feeling for musical rhythm shown by his pupils and he started to work on this problem.

He found that through experiencing rhythm physically in movement, his pupils gained a new understanding. What had been intellectual knowledge became a living experience that enriched their whole personality. It was the recreation of the old Greek concept of the unity of mind and body.

These years were a time of innovation in the arts, dance, the theatre, in medicine and education; Jaques-Dalcroze was among these innovators in the field of music education.

He soon found that there was much more in his ideas than just applying them to music students' problems. With doctors, psychiatrists and psychologists he began to explore the therapeutic possibilities of working through music and movement to find an answer to the questions he had asked himself.

"It was a question of replacing an intellectual with a sentient approach", wrote Andrew Loew, analysing the work of Jaques-Dalcroze.

Over the years many Dalcroze teachers in different countries working with doctors, psychiatrists and psychologists have specialised in and researched this therapeutic side of Dalcroze Eurhythmics (Music and Movement) known as psychomotricity, as it influences the whole person, mind and body.

Music used in this way has helped people with many different kinds of disabilities; the underlying ideas can be adapted to the needs of retarded children and adults, the special needs of the multiply handicapped, people in wheelchairs, the deaf and the blind, the mentally ill and geriatric patients; it can be used in day centres, residential institutions and hospitals.

This chapter aims to help movement therapists by introducing them to a way of using music in their treatment programmes that is stimulating and creative. It describes how the use of the structural elements of music become a guide and support to the patient, and a reinforcement in the treatment of dysfunction in movement.

No set patterns of movement or "exercises" are described, since in therapeutic work it is the therapist who decides what movement is necessary to attain a desired aim. The music acts as a global influence bringing sensitivity and freedom from inhibiting tensions.

The Uses of Music

Music has been used throughout the ages for many purposes. It plays an important part in ceremonial occasions and celebrations, in magical and religious rites and in healing. It was used to stimulate action, as in primitive dances, armies going into battle and the celebration of victories. These uses of music are historical facts and are illustrated in folklore, ancient ballads, songs and pageants.

Not only did music set the mood and feeling of the occasion, the movements of the participants were also in accord, as we see in the slow marching and solemn music of a funeral procession; occasions of public mourning or of public rejoicing were conducted with appropriate movement, gestures and music.

The Courtly dances, the Minuet, the Sarabande, the Gigue, the Allemande were played at certain speeds and demanded certain postures and steps – sometimes the costumes of the age imposed some restriction on the movement, but the union of the music and the movement was always there.

The folkdances held in the village and the fairs on the village green celebrated the seasons; the return of spring and the gathering of the harvest brought people together in singing and dancing.

Incantations and special words were used by doctor-priests in healing and for the exorcism of evil spirits. Traces of these ancient pagan rites can still be found in children's games and rhymes. Music and movement were the natural way in which people expressed their feelings. Music brought solace and comfort in bereavement and death and allowed grief to be openly expressed; it touched and influenced the whole personality and united people in common effort and feeling.

The music of today, especially pop music, occupies an important place in the life of young people; disco dancing seems to have its roots in the ritual dances of previous ages. It is a matter of debate whether the volume of sound and the insistent beat of the music penetrating the whole organism is beneficial or harmful. Does it create a wall of sound behind which people shelter and hide themselves from the realities of everyday life?

The impact of music on the whole organism can be pleasurable or shattering. What is there in music, this organisation of sound that has such influence on people, and how can it be used therapeutically?

The basic elements of music can be described as melody, rhythm, harmony, form. These elements can be presented and used in a simple and understandable way where movement "through music" is indicated for a remedial purpose. This may be for physical dysfunction or emotional difficulty that prevents the use of the body and expression of feeling in a normal and satisfying way; sensory and perceptual dysfunction may also be helped. Through the skill of the therapist in the use of the structural elements of music these disabilities may be mitigated if not eliminated.

There are many benefits, psychological as well as physical, to be derived from working in this way with movement and music: it induces relaxation after the stress of work and eases anxiety; it has been found to be beneficial in cardiac rehabilitation as it increases the intake of oxygen, and in cases of hypertension, as the feeling of well-being it induces leads to a lowering of blood pressure.

The presentation of this way of working can be in a group session or in an individual one-to-one session, depending on the needs, state, or age of the patient.

To stimulate interest in some age or ethnic groups, musical idioms of different countries and origins can be explored, for example, negro spirituals, work songs, sea shanties, dance rhythms and pop music. With some groups the remedial movements can be incorporated in a dramatic setting eg. a robot's actions, or moving parts of a machine, walking in space as a space-man. Stories in music such as the Negro Spiritual "Joshua fit de battle ob Jericho" can provide an exciting setting for many different movements and stimulate the participants' imaginations.

Children find real pleasure in working "through music" in their movement therapy sessions. They learn to listen and to feel and know their own bodies and are guided by the music in the performance of the desired movements. Music is flexible and is used as a material tailored to suit the customer and his particular needs.

Some children may need help in relating the movement desired by the therapist to themselves, and here music can act as a guide.

In these days of so much visual stimulation from television and often acting out of what they have seen, it seems that the response to aural stimulation 'doing what you hear' takes longer to understand, and descriptive words are necessary. It is a great help to say out loud what the music is telling you to do. Singing and moving helps to bring together mind and body.

Elderly patients and chronic psychotic patients can also find pleasure in this work. It can promote interaction and communication, especially if patients work in small groups or in pairs.

Patients who are not very active can use clapping — their own hands and those of their partner — instead of following the changes of speed through the walking and running; this also gives tactile contact with each other.

Using alternate limbs, the arms can show other changes in the music, such as changes of pitch loudness and softness. The partners can show the phrases by moving alternately either separately or holding hands.

The Basic Elements of Music

Melody, Rhythm, Harmony, Form – these four basic elements will be described, for the sake of clarity, as they have been used in a programme of Music and Movement therapy for children. Naturally in music these elements come together and create a whole, but in a therapeutic movement situation it is useful to consider them separately. The music examples are very simple and easy for children to understand and to show in movement that they have understood 'what the music is saying'.

With an appropriate presentation the work outlined is equally valid and adaptable to a basic programme for adult work; and with inventiveness and imagination on the part of the therapist can be developed to suit adult personalities and their needs.

Melody

Tunes, Nursery Rhymes, Songs, to be sung and for movement

Rhythm

This is first presented as changes of tempo or speed. Music does not stand still, it moves, it goes quickly, it goes slowly and there are many gradations of this quickness or slowness.

To follow these gradations the child can start by walking with the music; as it gets quicker he must run to keep up with it; if the music goes more and more slowly he must take longer and longer steps.

Musically this is represented by symbols of music notation, walking – crochet; running – quaver; slow – minim. These symbols are cut out of plywood and laid on the floor or on a table and the child must choose the one that fits what he has heard played.

So as well as the sense of hearing, the sense of sight is brought into play.

He must also discriminate and decide which of three possibilities he has heard and then take and move with the right symbol.

These symbols are then combined into a rhythmic phrase such as

He can say it, walk walk run run run run slow slow, clap it and say it, step it, clap it and say it. With increasing awareness, control and co-ordination these rhythmic phrases can become more complex involving faster steps 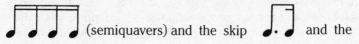 (semiquavers) and the skip and the

very slow **o** (semibreve).

So far these examples have been in a pulse or beat divisible by two and called simple time; and the stress when walking or running comes always on the same side of the body. However in music there is also the pulse divisible by three and called compound time so the stress comes on alternative sides of the body

These differences of stress can be felt and used by the therapist in the movements or the quality of the desired movement. At this stage, each note represents a step.

These cutout notes or symbols denoting minims

crotchets quavers

can be used in many ways, and many games using them can be invented that call for control and co-ordination. The sound accompaniment can be played on the piano or a tambour or drum.

Harmony

Tones of definite pitch (written vertically) sung or played together to form a chord. These chords concern the expressive side of music and give a distinctive feel to the melody they accompany.

Phrasing and Form

Arrangement or style of a musical composition, in which melody, rhythm and harmony combine to create a whole design.

A musical composition is built up of phrases, as a poem is built up of lines and into a verse. These phrases expand and develop into a complete form. This form or design can be built also in movement.

For a therapeutic aim, say, movement of hands and arms, a tune that could be a useful guide is "Frère Jacques" in which each short phrase is made up of two exactly repeated bars, so each movement made for instance on the right side of the body must be repeated exactly on the left side.

To reinforce the child's body image, instead of using the words of the song, he can sing which part of himself he is moving.

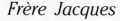

Frère Jacques

Frère Jacques, Frère Jacques, dormez vous, dormez vous,

walk/ w/ w/ w/   w/ w/ w/ w   w/ w/ slow   w/ w/ slow

sonnez les matines sonnez les matines, Ding din don. Ding din don.

run/ r/ r/ r/ w/   w/   r/ r/ r/ r/ w/ w/   w/ w/ slow   w/ w/ slow

Movement Shape and Design

Many folksong melodies can be used for drawing in space round the child. Painting, following the phrases, on a large sheet of paper on the floor, or using coloured chalks on a blackboard. If the blackboard is on a wall the child can move as he draws which gives very interesting shapes and dynamic nuance to the patterns created. Either hand, or both together can be freely used which stimulates creativity and imagination. The child can also sing or make noises as he moves and draws.

The movement is supported by the musical phrases and the child becomes conscious of the space travelled by his hand or arm or whole body and that it is not just a displacement from A to B. The movement may be regulated by the loudness or softness and the speed of the music.

In a piece of music in which there are contrasting phrases, these can be shown by orchestrating the design by using different limbs and parts of the body.

This bodily orchestration can be accompanied by using different instruments, tuned or untuned percussion, and is very effective. The starting position in space can be from standing, sitting or lying down which will stimulate movement imagination.

The sense of time and the feeling for space can be developed by using Rounds and Canons such as London's Burning etc. with patients in small groups, each group entering into movement at the correct musical moment – the distance covered in space being governed by the length of the tune, the number of the phrases and the speed at which it is taken.

The amount of energy expended to fit the character of the tune must be felt for a sensitive response to be forthcoming. Moving to a tune in this way brings a sense of order and discipline and an acceptance of a framework into which the design or pattern must fit.

The Architecture of a Musical Composition

1 Accent

This is the regularly recurring stress on the first of a predetermined grouping of pulses. This grouping is known as bar times.

$$2\overset{>}{} -|\overset{>}{} -|\overset{>}{} -|\overset{>}{} -\| \quad 3\overset{>}{} - -|\overset{>}{} - -|\overset{>}{} - -|\overset{>}{} - -\|$$

$$4\overset{>}{} - - -|\overset{>}{} - - -|\overset{>}{} - - -|\overset{>}{} - - -\|$$

2 Anacrusis, Crusis, Metacrusis.
Preparation, Action, Relaxation.

In music as in movement there must be a preparation or anticipation. A physical action needs a preparation time. This may be very rapid as in fear or flight, or a longer time of consideration, as in choosing which chocolate to take from a choice of flavours. Then follows the period of relaxation, relief or satisfaction after the action.

Musically this is ANACRUSIS, CRUSIS, METACRUSIS; the anacrusis is the unaccented note or notes leading to the accent and the launching of the tune on its way. Some tunes do not have this anacrusis, the action or crusis starts at once, so the preparation must be internally organised, the tune then pursues its course until the final cadence or end.

ANACRUSIC
Londonderry Air

CRUSIC
Good King Wenceslas

3 The Interval

The interval, the distance between notes in a melody is an important guide to movement. Do the sounds come in leaps or smaller steps? What do the intervals suggest in the way of energy? Do they go up or down in pitch? What do they express in feeling?

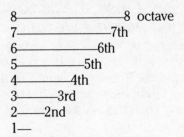

Ex. 1. Two part Invention – J S Bach

Intervals rising from lower note of the octave.

Ex. 2. "La fille aux cheveux de lin" Prelude – C. Debussy.

Intervals falling from higher note of octave.

These two contrasting themes show how the placing of intervals convey different moods and therefore influence movement, energy and feeling. The one uses leaping 3rds, 5th and 8th (octave); the other falling and rising 3rds within the octave.

Ex.3 SAINT PAUL'S STEEPLE.   Traditional

Up-on Paul's steeple stands a tree, as full of apples as may be. The

litt -le boys of London Town, They run with hooks to pull them down, and

Then they run from hedge to hedge un- til they come to London Bridge.

A tune with contrasting phrases of scale passages and phrases of intervals. Suggested movement could be running and leaping.

4 Rests and Silences

In music there are various symbols replacing notes that denote cessation of sound for shorter or longer periods. Although the sound has momentarily stopped, the pulse of the music must be carried on internally during the time of silence so that the sound is taken up again at the correct place.

In movement this silence would be cessation of movement, but equally this stillness must be thought through, and the movement resumed at the correct moment.

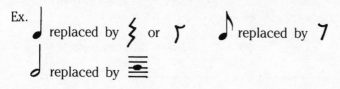

Ex.

5 Nuance

(A) DYNAMIC NUANCE. Gradations of changes of loudness and softness in the music — shown in words and signs.

(B) AGOGIC NUANCE. Gradations of changes of speed in the music — shown by notations and words. These nuances have their counterpart in movement through changes in energy and speed.

Musical Words or Sign	Corresponding Movements
(A) DYNAMIC NUANCE (ENERGY)	
CRESCENDO – getting louder	Increase of tension – scope of movement
DIMINUENDO– getting softer	Decrease of tension – reduction of movement
Forte, fortissimo – Loud, very loud (f, ff)	Big strong movements
Piano, Pianissimo – Soft, very soft (p, pp)	Small soft movements
Legato – smoothly	Flowing movements
Staccato – detached playing	Crisp, sharp movements
(B) AGOGIC NUANCE (SPEED)	
Accelerando – getting faster	Slow stepping to fast running
Ritardando – getting slower	Fast running to slow stepping
Presto – fast	Light, quick movement
Moderato – moderate easy speed	Easy movement
Lento or Largo – slow	Heavy slow movement

Playing Musical Instruments

For the purposes of remedial movement through music, the playing of an instrument can be an added incentive to good and correct use of the body.

The following are easily obtainable suitable instruments.

Musical Use	Instrument	Therapeutic Application
(1) Wind		
Melody	Recorders Bamboo pipes Flutes Melodicas Harmonicas	Co-ordination of breathing. Tongue and finger dexterity. Co-ordination of eye and ear in reading the music and production of correct sound. Good body posture, sitting and standing.
(2) Plucked Stringed Instruments		
Accompaniments to Voice	Lyre Small harps Guitar Mandolin Banjo Auto harp	Position of hand. Finger dexterity. Ease of arm and shoulder movement. Co-ordination of the two hands.
(3) Tuned Percussion		
Melody Accompaniments to voice and wind	Glockenspiel Xylophone Chime bars Metalophone Tubular bells	Wrist and hand movements with the rebound so that the note can 'sing' (difficult for some children). Spacing of sound and pitch. Co-ordination of eye and ear.

(4) Untuned Percussion

Rhythm	Drums Tambours Tambourines Chinese blocks	Sensitive use of hand with sticks, or with hands and fingers without sticks. Sensitive wrist work with beater.

(5) Cymbals

Dynamic effects Dramatic effects	Cymbals, small medium and large	Sweeping cymbals past each other (arm and shoulder movements). Swept round on floor different tone colour. Two cymbals swept round and round each other.
	Single cymbal held by thong	Played with beater in other hand, using head or stick on edge of cymbal.
	Large cymbal on stand.	Free movement in space, following duration of sound. Test of keenness of hearing.
	Chinese gong	Free movement (vibrations can be overwhelming to young children).

(6) Piano

MELODY AND RHYTHM. The piano is an instrument upon which all basic elements can be played, all dynamic nuances explored and music played for listening, moving and enjoyment.

(7) The Voice

A person's voice and body are his first instruments, they are part of him. With his voice he can create sounds to accompany his movements and his movements can create improvised vocalisation.

Improvised vocal sounds and improvised movements can create communication and interaction between individuals and groups.

In using these instruments attention must be paid to their *timbre*, that is, the quality of the different sounds of wind, stringed, or percussion, as their different sounds influence movement in subtle ways. Some may be pleasing and bring enjoyment and outgoing reactions; others may be actively disliked and cause withdrawal and the blocking out of the sounds.

Non-Musical Aids

It can be very helpful to use non-musical aids within a musical context; for example, fairly large gaily coloured balls and hoops, canes, pieces of rope, a short length of ¼ square catapult elastic, different coloured chiffon scarves. These encourage freedom in movement and stimulate imaginative patterns and designs.

Movement Context	Musical Context
(1) Balls	
Bouncing and catching Throwing and catching	Music in low notes on piano Music in high notes on piano
Rolling with hands and arms – flowing movement – away from the body.	"I saw three ships come sailing by" – *Ex. 1.*
Spinning – fingers and hand – crisp concentrated movement. Close to the body.	"Twinkle, twinkle, little star" – *Ex. 2.*

Ex. 1.
"I Saw Three Ships"

Ex. 2.
"Twinkle, twinkle little star"

(2) Hoops

Free swinging movements
Rolling with hands.

(3) Canes

Stepping – tapping on
1st beat of bar

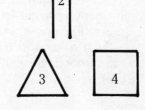

Match bar time
played 2, 3, 4, to pattern

(4) Ropes

Free designs made on
the floor, followed in
movement, on the floor
or in space.

Improvised music melodic or percussion.

(5) Elastics

Work with a partner
Leader and follower.
Following or resisting.

Moving with phrases of
a tune

(6) Scarves

Free movements in
space

Improvised music or
voice.

Making and Playing

For the patient to make his own instrument and then to play it is a wonderful and for some a very therapeutic experience.

The Bamboo Pipe in particular can give this experience. It is the owner's own creation and becomes a most cherished possession. This is very true for patients in an institution where personal possessions may be few.

The individual makes, he plays (uses what he has made), he has great enjoyment and he is in communication with his fellows.

In the making of an instrument, the pipe, xylophone or drum many different levels are called into play and also the co-ordination of eye, ear, and hands.

Such a session could well be part of an occupational therapy programme and brings another dimension to movement through music.

Application — Special Groups

Severely Subnormal

Work in the way already described especially with the notes and balls is very successful with patients with an I.Q. between 20–30, and very limited or no proper speech. The patients have something to hold that they can see and feel that acts as a focus of attention.

With the notes the therapist will at first have to move with the group using a tambour to keep the different speeds moving, and saying or singing what they are doing.

We are walk-ing walking walking walking all a-round.

We go run run etc. We go slow-ly etc.

Patients with an I.Q. 20–30 may not get very much further than this.

Those with an I.Q. 40–50+ can do more advanced work with the notes, clapping and stepping a short rhythmic phrase, making up their own rhythmic pattern for stepping; analyse it and write it on a blackboard. Conducting moving groups of notes is much enjoyed.

In trying to improve general movement with severely subnormal people caution must be used as words are not always understood and body image is very weak so any criticism may inhibit movement altogether. Improvement comes through their pleasure in this work and the lessening of anxiety.

The balls are good for co-ordination, throwing and catching, bouncing and catching, while running or skipping. The concept of high and low can also be brought in.

Very sensitive and musical responses can come when using the 'spinning tune' and the 'rolling tune'. This sensitivity of response is one of the principal aims in many of the ideas suggested.

Severely Disabled

Very physically handicapped or non-ambulant patients can respond to and use these ideas. For example, when a drum is strategically placed where an athetoid arm and hand will hit it anyhow, the patient can then take part in a band group.

A very spastic patient unable to move his arms or use his hands can play a big cymbal on a stand in front of him. A soft beater is inserted into his clenched fist, and a helper supports his arm from the elbow and gently lets the beater play the cymbal. This patient too is then a member of the band group, often to his great joy, and he is actively participating in a group situation.

In such a group the therapist could play a pipe or recorder to lead or make the melody and let the 'percussionists' make a 'free' accompaniment. She can also move from one player to another and play directly to and with him.

Wheelchair patients can manoeuvre their chairs around and 'dance' to the music. This moving with the music is much enjoyed by geriatric patients, especially to old and familiar tunes.

With ingenuity many ways of moving with music can be found.

Autism

It is well known that autistic people respond to music to a

remarkable degree. It somehow penetrates their isolation and they become absorbed in the music they hear.

It may be more difficult to get them to move with the music; it does not always seem to stimulate spontaneous movement. Their hyperactivity, unpredictable behaviour and disregard for people around them makes group work hard to achieve.

With these patients movement should be interpreted in a wide sense, eg. a smile of pleasure or a relaxation of tension show that they have reacted and felt a contact with something outside themselves.

The Blind and the Deaf

The needs of these two special groups must each be studied in depth. Much work and research has been done by Dalcroze teachers for blind and for deaf people, and ways found of using the work in music and movement previously described have helped to bring them into the world of the sighted and the hearing.

For blind people the music as a guide to movement can help mobility and orientation in space and could be of value in a rehabilitation programme.

For deaf people the clues to the music could be visual; the therapist models the musical changes and tactile clues are received through the fingers feeling the vibrations of different instruments.

Response and Achievement

Case I

A woman who suffered from cerebral palsy (spasticity) at birth was profoundly deaf and because of this had little speech. When attending the Social Services Day Centre she joined a "Music and Movement" group. In the early days it was difficult to understand what she was saying and almost impossible to hold a conversation.

At this time she was 26 years of age, small and bent, but

able to walk with elbow crutches. She was pretty and possessed a lovely smile. Her progress was spectacular over a period of years. She gained much confidence as her ability to communicate with others showed and speech became much clearer. During this time her elbow crutches were raised on three occasions to keep pace with her growth in stature. She had an innate sense of rhythm and excelled at the exercises to music as well as having great mastery of rhythmical beating on her drum. Unfortunately she had to leave the District to live with her sister which was a great loss to us all at the Day Cente.

(Pam Hook, Medau/Dalcroze/ADT.Dip.)

Case II

In a big hospital for the severely subnormal a group of young and late teenage boys working through this method of Dalcroze Eurhythmics (Music and Movement) over a number of years came to a state of awareness and responsiveness in this situation which gave them pleasure, a feeling of achievement and responsibility that was remarkable.

The sensitivity of response of many of them, especially in the ball exercises done on the floor was especially noticeable; the spinning and rolling of the ball following spontaneously the changes of speed and dynamics played on the piano gave moments of real beauty and total involvement with the music. Their growing ability in physical adaptation to the various musical commands showed an increasing awareness, and better self control and co-ordination.

The members of the group naturally changed over the years, but as new ones joined, the old ones absorbed them and the unheeding and stereotyped movements changed and became more harmonious.

Progress in work with people in such a hospital situation where experiences are limited cannot be measured by the time scale of an ordinary school programme. Improvement comes through the happiness this work seems to bring to the individual, with the consequent freeing of physical and emotional tensions. This makes possible movement experiences which can lead to imaginative and creative movement, related, whenever possible, to things that extend their knowledge of life outside the usual pattern on the wards. This everyday hospital life is now happily becoming more interesting and many of the residents have in themselves more to draw on.

These wider experiences can be reinforced by the use of stories in the music and movement sessions as was demonstrated by this group of teenage boys who gave a most realistic and alive performance of "Joshua fit de battle ob Jericho". All the music and movement work done so far, changes of speed, dynamics, phrasing and form, was brought together in this story. The words were sung by a member of staff and shown in movement by the group; the necessary instruments, with some additions, were also played by the boys themselves. The only staff participation was from the singer and the pianist.

This is but one example of the response, achievement and sense of identity gained through music and movement used as a group therapy experience for teenage boys resident in hospital.

Case III

This was a group of adult men and women resident in a unit for mentally handicapped people. The disabilities of this group are not specifically physical conditions needing special remedial treatment. They are all mobile and aged between 25 and 45 years; but all have difficulty in adapting themselves and their movements to the dictates of the music, eg. changes of speed. They have a set stereotyped tempo of their own which is hard to alter, so the aim of the exercises given is to bring self awareness and the ability to relate their movements to what is going on musically.

One young woman, prone to periods of withdrawal into herself but who has clearly been listening and has understood "what the music says" has this difficulty of physical adaptation, so having to show in movement what she has heard brings her back for a time into reality.

Two young men listening and observing from "the side lines" may suddenly hurl themselves round the room in active participation in the more vigorous exercises of running and skipping.

Although it is difficult to get any awareness of group feeling with these very different personalities with unpredictable behaviour, the very obvious pleasure this work gives them makes it well worth while.

Conclusion

It must be understood that this chapter is not an exposition of Music Therapy as such, since this book concerns Movement Therapy.

This chapter describes a way of using music through Dalcroze Eurhythmics (Music and Movement) in a treatment programme devised by the movement therapist for specific or general psycho-motor dysfunction. It aims to show the therapist who may not be a trained musician how to use live music and the things in musical structure that must be considered and understood for music and movement to become integrated.

The musical examples are illustrations of these points, and with inventiveness and imagination the therapist will find ways of using them, and finding or improvising similar musical guides. For improvised music the tuned and untuned percussion instruments are especially useful and effective.

Live music, however simple, is much more telling than tapes or records. A live contact between patient, therapist and the music can be maintained and instantly adapted to an unforeseen occurrence in the course of a session. This is not so when only tapes or records are used, as once started, the tape or record cannot be changed or adapted.

There are of course times when some particular theme in a musical composition is relevant and useful. An example could be the sudden dramatic accents contrasting and breaking into the calmer periods of the Pastoral Symphony of Beethoven (No. 6).

Too much use of recorded music may degenerate into just 'music going on' during treatment; it may not be under the therapist's control. With live music the patient can be kept in a state of alertness and expectation since live music and improvisation *are* under the therapist's control. She must play with an alive touch that conveys the movement, and she herself must feel the movement and the quality of the movement that she wants through her whole attitude and voice.

Playing for movement is not the same as just playing the piano, or any other instrument. The simplest musical improvisation that really fits the movement is far more effective than attempting a lot of more elaborate piano playing.

The patient, child or adult needs the opportunity to improvise for himself on the different instruments and to express his own feelings and creativity. The demands made in this work on the patient (child or adult) are that 'he does what he hears', and calls for attentive listening, concentration, discrimination, self control, co-ordination, self awareness and awareness of others. Through this work imagination and creativity are stimulated and fostered. With growing confidence and sensitivity of response the whole personality is influenced and enriched and mind and body brought into harmony.

Bibliography

Dutoit, C. L., *Music Movement Therapy*, Dalcroze Society, Inc., B. M. Dalcroze, London WC1V 6XX

Alvin, J., *Music Therapy*, John Clare Books, 106 Cheyne Walk, London SW10 0JR

Bailey, P., *They Can Make Music*, Oxford University Press (Adaptation of instruments to patient needs)

Roberts, R., *Instruments Made To Be Played*, Dryad Press, Leicester (Instructions and plans for making)

The Pipers Guild Handbook, The Pipers Guild, 11 Lambourn Way, Tunbridge Wells, Kent TN2 5HJ (Instructions for making)

Campbell, L., *Sketching At The Keyboard*, Stainer and Bell, London

Miroslaw Janiszewski, *Le Rhythme 1979*, Federation International des Enseignants de Rhythmique

INFORMATION, TRAINING — FOR MUSIC THERAPY:
British Society for Music Therapy
B.S.M.T. Administrator
Guildhall School of Music and Drama
Barbican, London EC2Y 8DT

FOR DALCROZE EURHYTHMICS:
The Secretary
The Dalcroze Society Inc
26 Bullfinch Road
Selsdon Vale
South Croydon CR2 8PW

CHAPTER 4

THE THERAPEUTIC VALUE
OF
MOVEMENT AND DANCE

By Chloe Gardner and Audrey Wethered

Introduction

Dance has been used as a healing art for many thousands of years, though in the developed world its virtues have been largely neglected and its practice forgotten.

Since the 1930s, occupational therapists have used social dancing in psychiatric hospitals. This usually included folk dance, and often remedial or 'keep fit' exercises were required.

One of the authors started in this way in the 1940s, and she found that:–

a)	The physical state reflected the psychological condition.

b)	Treating one helped to reach the other, but

c)	Directly corrective exercises were unsuccessful because they disregarded the psychological reasons for the physical state, and the patients could not co-operate. She sought other approaches and found that experience of Laban's work gave her a deep enough understanding of movement to be able to redesign exercises, to encourage fuller participation by the patients.

Meanwhile, Jungian psychotherapists were extending their use of the arts to include dance, notably at the Withymead Centre in Devonshire. The other author's work has been mainly in this field. Her initial approach through music revealed the rich possibilities of communication in movement, and led her to train at the Laban Studio.

Dance

Dance is defined here as: a creative, artistic discipline involving the whole person: body, intellect, imagination, emotion and spirit. It is both expressive and receptive, communicating the dancer's feelings, and changing and resolving them in relation to other people or the environment.

It is clear that the limited type of technique or 'body drill' that some sophisticated dance styles demand is not what the authors visualise in this context, as the therapeutic approach is creative, exploratory and experiential.

Creative dance is never a 'soft option', just jiggling about to repetitive music, nor subjugating the body to a set of rules while neglecting the intellect and the psyche. The dancer/patient may be asked to answer challenges, eg. to produce his own variations on a movement idea, develop this into a phrase, remember it, adapt it to a partner's work, or fit it into a group effort. He will have to think for himself and make decisions. Discovering co-ordination and personal rhythm, management of body weights, gaining awareness of his centre and increasing his expressive ability demand attention and concentration. Even so, there is still room for enjoyment, and certainly for fulfilment!

Therapy

This word is often loosely used nowadays, and dance has so many beneficial aspects that there is sometimes confusion over the distinction between recreation, exercise, social dance, educational dance and the treatment of pathological states. It is with this latter definition that this chapter is concerned. The healing process is discussed in the section on psychotherapy.

The Therapist

Some experienced dance therapists work autonomously and are responsible to the doctor(s) in charge of the patients referred to them. Others work under physiotherapists or occupational therapists. They are responsible for their patients' safety as well as their treatment and will be expected to ensure that patients leave sessions in a reasonably tranquil condition.

The dance therapist should respect the boundaries of her profession and not trespass into the field of psychotherapy, in which she is not qualified. She should have sufficient understanding of herself to enable her to observe objectively, and to avoid using the dance session for the gratification of her own unconscious needs. She must co-operate as a full member of the treatment team. She must prepare herself, rather than the session material, by dancing for her own enjoyment and experience. Having gathered all possible information about the patients she expects to be treating, she must bring to the forefront of her mind her knowledge of movement principles and analysis. The theme she uses to keep cohesion and continuity throughout the session can be developed in a variety of ways by stressing different aspects of movement according to the immediate needs and abilities she observes in the patients.

Notation

Benesh and Laban both devised systems of notating dances, to record the choreography in order that future dancers could learn and perform the dances created. Symbols are used to define the steps, positions, body parts, grouping and correlation of the dancers, and the time and phrasing relative to the music. In addition Laban invented what he called 'Effort Notation' which denotes the quality of movement, the expressive content that can convey moods, emotions, actions in all the variation of the dance and what it demands. Also he devised symbols for the shaping of the body. These symbols are classified under 'general theory'.

The following are contrasting examples of the use of Effort Notation in observation. They show the ways two different people rise out of a chair.

A) _ ∠ < ⌐ > ∠ ⁄ ∅

B) ↓ ∠ ⌣ ⌐

a) denotes the difficulty an old person has in rising.
b) denotes the ease with which a younger person makes the same action.

This Effort and Shaping Notation is also of immense value in learning to observe objectively, noting the individual variations in the qualities – increase and decrease, expanding and shrinking, acceleration and retardation, and how the elements of movement interweave. Therapists can use this notation when assessing a patient's personality, problems, mood and potential. During a dance session, this discipline of objective observation enables the therapist/leader to monitor the patient's needs and modify the programme accordingly.

General Theory

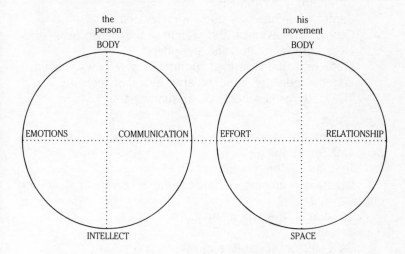

These two diagrams, if superimposed, sum up the holistic approach that movement offers to the therapist. Movement, as it is fashioned and disciplined into dance, can help to integrate the whole person. Movement is the common factor in all activity and is as individual as handwriting (which is frozen movement).

In any kind of sickness a person's personal rhythms can be disturbed, making co-ordination, communication and practical tasks difficult, and causing emotional distress. The dynamics of these personal rhythms can be rediscovered through dance, which is adaptable to individual needs. The way we move is determined by our physique and personality, but habitual ways of moving also affect our mood, health, behaviour and response to challenges. The analysis of movement described by Rudolf Laban is an excellent structure on which to base a therapeutic technique, and an abstraction of some of the features of his work relevant to therapy follows. It will be seen that physical and psychological aspects are inseparable in this work.

There are four main principles of movement:

The Body

STRUCTURE:

Symmetry – Asymmetry.

Centre of lightness – the thoracic area.

Centre of heaviness and weight – the pelvic area.

Head, limbs, centre and periphery

Surfaces – flat, rounded, pointed (eg. elbows, heels).

Edges – edge of hand or arm, sides of feet etc.

The body as a whole, or as many parts.

FUNCTION:

Locomotion: weight transference, swaying, rolling, crawling, walking, running.

Jumping, falling, turning.

Opening — closing, curling around the centre or stretching out.

Twisting – the whole or parts.

Stability.

Balance, both stable and labile.

Whole body shaping.

Gesture: one or more parts moving alone, or in relation to the whole, or each other.

Initiation of a movement from the centre to the periphery, or in reverse.

Simultaneous or successive movement – the whole moving at once or one part moving after another.

Movement memory, and concept.

Effort

The dynamic qualities of movement are not only concerned with practical actions, they are expressive and vital to any kind of communication.

The elements of effort and the symbols used in notation are:

Space (focus)	variation between the extremes of – Flexibility . . . and . . . Directness
Weight (force)	variation between the extremes of – Fine touch . . . and . . . Strength (lightness)

Time	variation between the extremes of –	
___/	Sustainment . . . and . . . Suddenness	/__
	(legato) , (staccato)	

Flow (control)	variation between the extremes of –	
___/	Freedom . . . and . . . Control	L__
	(abandon) (bound)	

People have different attitudes to these elements according to their personalities and mood, and this gives rise to different personal rhythms.

It is the ability to vary these qualities which makes a movement harmonious, relaxed and flowing. The reader should try to count the number of times s/he varies each one of the elements as he lifts a cup of coffee to his lips, or puts on his clothes.

In functional movements flow is seldom free; there is nearly always some measure of control. Free flow can be experienced in water by those without fear of water, hence the importance of water play for children, as they develop from an almost entirely flow state into an adult who can vary all the components of effort. Exaggeration of bound flow is often seen in someone attempting a difficult task. It inhibits the establishment of a rhythmic phrase, by making other variations more difficult, and it creates unease in the performer. Disturbance of flow can be seen in any movement and even in the quality of stillness, and may give some indication of subsequent behaviour.

Space

General space is the three-dimensional space of the working area, its height, width, and all levels. It involves filling the space or shrinking from it; the concept of near-to and far-away; pathways – on the floor, in the air, curving, angular, straight, zig-zag, diagonal etc.; concept of patterns – eg. circles, triangles, lines; place, finding one's place in space, establishing it, leaving it, returning to it, and finally travelling through space.

We can organise our bodies through spaces, and follow directions, even with our eyes shut, and from memory. Most people can judge whether a space is big enough for them to get through. This all requires a concept, memory or imagination of space. Patterns can be seen and memorised, eg. following a map, and then danced or moved. We even extend this ability into handling objects, eg. the supermarket trolley has to be steered through throngs of shoppers, or the car driven through three-dimensional space as underpasses, flyovers and round-abouts are negotiated.

Personal space is the area close around oneself. If one reaches out with arms, legs and spine extended, one can define one's own kinaesphere. Wherever one goes in general space, one's kinaesphere goes with one, and one's movement within it is individual and is expressive and practical.

The structure of the kinaesphere is:

1. DIMENSIONS

a) The high–deep axis, connecting the area high above the head with the body centre and the feet and supporting ground. It relates to the effort element of

b) The forward–backward axis, connecting the area far out in front, through the centre with the area far behind. The future and the past. A medium level, horizontal line. It relates to the element of

c) The narrow–wide axis, connecting the area on one side of the body with that on the other, through the centre. One side can feel narrow as it crosses the centre, or open as it extends to its own side. It relates to the effort element of

Awareness of the dimensional cross, or centre, makes it possible to stretch away from the centre and balance and return to the centre. For a movement to have power or impact it must come from the centre. The centre is at the crux of emotional experience.

2. THE PLANES

a) The horizontal plane ('table' plane). A skater spins around the high–deep axis, and the turning happens in the horizontal plane, linking the extremes of the other two dimensions.

Symbols: Expansion | Contraction

                                          //   //⁻

b) The vertical ('door') plane. A cartwheel turns around the forward–backward axis and happens in the vertical plane, linking the extremes of the other two dimensions.

Symbols: Expansion |//   Contraction //

                                                                  |

c) The sagital ('wheel') plane. A somersault turns around the narrow–wide axis and happens in the sagital plane, linking the extremes of the other two dimensions.

Symbols: Expansion   //   Contraction //

                                         _   _

These gymnastic turns are mentioned only to identify the planes simply. Their performance requires expansion and contraction in the appropriate plane. All the shaping movements of our bodies require a similar but less dramatic growing and shrinking in one or more of the planes of space, eg. getting out of a car, into a bath, or into a crowded train.

The planes are also connected with communication, presentation and commitment. The way a person shapes his body, expanding or contracting in any plane, the fact that he avoids using one plane altogether, or only creates gestures rather than whole body movements in any one plane, tells us a good deal about his personality and his potential. Experience of growing and shrinking in any plane, or of rotating in that plane, tends to establish more strongly the axis around which the rotation is made, eg. opening–closing, spinning, or rotating in the horizontal plane accentuates the high–deep axis (or dimension) so improving self-awareness and balance.

3. THE DIAGONALS

These are also imaginary lines from the centre outward, leading the dancer between the extremities of the dimensions into experiences of instability.

Relationship

This includes relationship to oneself ie. body awareness

and awareness of the kinaesphere; extending to partners, trios and groups, and the experiencing of different roles within the partnership or group ie. leading–following, showing–copying, simultaneously, in cannon or in sequence. Playing one's part in a team ie. group improvisation, and helping to form choreographic shapes with a group. It also involves attention to the accompaniment; percussion, music, or words and appreciation of the environment.

A phrase has a start and finish, with one or more highlights between. This is true of dance phrases and also of actions such as putting on boots, or combing the hair. What holds a movement phrase together is the relationship of effort and shape variations within the action. This gives the action its rhythm. A lack of this kind of relationship and flow indicates some co-ordination problem, which may be psychological, physical or neurological, and which causes the subject to feel frustration in practical and expressive tasks.

From the natural links between the components of effort and the dimensions of space, and their influence on emotional expression and practical actions, it can be seen that dance is a treatment approach which can be either direct or roundabout, according to the patient's abilities and tolerance of stress or pain.

Treatment of Psychiatric Disorders

Workers in this field will recognise much of the theory as written in the section on general theory. Movement is not only expressive of the mover, but it also affects him. We cannot alter basic personality, but carefully graded movement experience can help the subject to grow; to strengthen his weaker abilities, and so overcome some of his problems and come to terms with others.

Our bodies tell us what we need: rest, exercise, stretching, curling up and hiding away, discipline, concentration, etc. People who are out of tune with their bodies are unaware of these needs and go on building up tensions and fatigue, or anger and frustration. It is possible to recognise these needs in patients and to lead them from what they think they want into the sort of experience they really need.

Pure dance gives the patient deep inner experience because it needs no words and does not externalise the participation by the use of imagery or role-playing. Feelings and their associated actions serve the development of the dance, and they can be tackled and integrated in this context. The discipline of the art of dance makes a safe framework for the exploration of life situations and relationships, without verbal discussion, unless it is clearly indicated. Unacceptable behaviour can be canalised into artistic work which, if repeated, can give the patient confidence that he can direct his negative feelings safely. The aim of treatment is different for each patient and his programme has to be tailored to fit. Movement observation of the patient as he enters the room will reveal how the principal symptoms are manifested in movement, and indicate the best way to lead him to extend and vary his movement patterns. It also gives insight into what would otherwise be unpredictable behaviour.

Much of the session time has to be spent in "sugaring the pill", since to make demands on a patient which attack his illness directly, could be traumatic, unless many easier ways of working are suggested as well, eg. if a patient has a particular difficulty in opening out in the horizontal plane, then over-stressing this action would be too traumatic, would cause tension and perhaps even some outburst, or refusal to attend again, and the patient would withdraw even more. The problem might be better approached through a) Effort, using play between the flexible and direct qualities, or b) Body, increasing self awareness and confidence, or c) Space, using dimensions and establishing the high–deep axis, and the horizontal plane.

Many sick people have difficulty in the variation of effort elements, and so cannot express their feelings easily. They are living in a kind of straight-jacket. If this is suddenly removed and the pent-up feelings allowed to emerge, without being contained in a structured activity such as dance, the patient may be overwhelmed and will need much confidence in the therapist's ability. It is well to remember that catharsis needs form.

Practice

Here are some examples of how the dance therapist would aim to work, within the above limits, when treating some of the common problems seen in psychiatric illness.

1. Poor Self-awareness and blurred Ego Boundaries.
Body awareness.
Group sensitivity.
Spatial Orientation.
Body parts moving in relation to each other.
Whole body action – locomotion, rolling, jumping, pausing, turning, balance and the carriage of the body weight.
Personal Space, dimensions.
Group and partner work.

2. Relationship Difficulties
As above, plus:
Awareness of self.
Partner work, group improvisation. Various partner relationships, leading, following, simultaneous improvisation, working in cannon etc.
Work on the planes, particularly the horizontal.
Effort: check the patient's ability to communicate and control his feelings.

3. Poor Initiative, decision-making and choice.
Solo improvisation.
Leadership.
Self valuation. Awareness of self and of the body centre, encouraging movements to come from the centre into the periphery.
Improvisation, with progressively less direction, and involving the kinaesphere, and effort.
Effort element of time and the sagital plane. Work to music and using percussion.
Clear start and finish to phrases.

4. Poor Concentration, poor perseverance.
Construction of a dance improvisation, repetition and

fashioning of a finished product.

Work on dimensions, particularly high–deep and forward–backward.

Effort: elements of weight and time.

Use of music. Not repetitive, but music which has to be attended to.

5. Non Integration of Emotions:
Communication difficulties.

Sensitive use of dynamics (Effort).

Body awareness.

Group sensitivity. Effort: variations in all elements.

Rhythm: swing, balance, impulse (where the climax starts the action) and impact (where the climax comes at the end).

Attention to phrasing.

Improvisation with partners or trios.

6. Overwhelming Fantasy.

Self awareness, Body awareness.

Concentration.

Relationship to others, the work room, the floor, music, and the construction of the dance.

Use of personal space, particularly dimensions.

Orientation in general space (area).

Technical work with body.

Work with partner, lead–follow.

Group work.

Dance activity rather than mime.

Use of objects to dance with, eg. tambourine or scarf, percussion instrument, ball.

Work on themes sufficiently difficult to demand concentration and intellectual effort.

Music chosen needs to be well structured.

7. Depression.

To encourage effort elements of lightness, flexibility and acceleration.

Work on body awareness.

Group work.

Use of space (area) fully, stressing the higher levels, the high–deep dimension.

Work on the effort element of weight, using strength and heaviness as a preparation for lightness and elevation.

All work on lightness and quickness must be a by-product of the heaviness and weight which the patient feels. A patient with depression needs to find a positive use for his downward pressing characteristic posture.

Practice Groups

Members of a dance group may experience the session material at different levels. Some may enjoy it as a "fun" happening. Others may be deeply involved in their relationship to themselves and to the world. Some may be developing self-control, while others are enjoying the freedom to invent movement sequences and to express themselves. Some may use their energies entirely physically, shunning creative and communicative tasks, perhaps because they are not ready to probe into their problems, or are unwilling or unable to commit themselves totally and cannot focus their energies. Understanding the patient's pathology and observing his mood enables the therapist to know when to encourage X to participate at a deeper level, or to help Y to find the way to a less demanding experience. Elements of human relationship such as domination, submission, restriction, responsibility, tolerance etc., can be experienced bodily and emotionally through group dance.

It is useful to know the ethnic and cultural symbolism in the forms of group dance, and to be aware of the opposite and negative significance which participation may arouse in sick people. Choreographic group forms such as blocks, wedges, and tangles, will affect different people in different ways, according to their position in the group, their individual illness, and relationship with other group members. Good management of these situations can be a valuable part of treatment.

The 'warm-up' or 'tune-up' in a group session depends upon the state of the group and their needs at the moment. The therapist will lead them towards the concentration and co-operation needed for the type of dance-work she knows will benefit them. Thus it will be understood that there can be no rigid programme, but a theme which allows for many different interpretations will help to give a feeling of continuity.

A group might arrive in a highly excited state, wanting to shout and stamp, and unaware of any other need. If this continues without guidance, the mood will build up into a dangerously aggressive one in some people, frightening themselves and others and providing no satisfaction. The stamping and shouting would be organised into a group effort, using a common rhythm, and as soon as this is achieved, changes in intensity, rhythm and spatial pathways will be needed to contain the energy and absorb possible aggression. This will help group members to see that there is a way of coping with their nearly uncontrollable moods, and they are usually glad to be released and helped to experience a different set of feelings. They would then be ready for more demanding treatment work.

Another group might arrive in a negative state, only wanting to curl up and withdraw. In this case the session must start more gently; maybe with the carriage of body weight, balance, sway and awareness of the centre. Exploration of the dimensions would be helpful; examination of personal space, leading into general space, and meetings with others, would prepare the group for the work on effort needed for communication.

These examples are only one way of handling such groups. Exactly how a therapist works depends on her sensitivity and her on-going assessment of the group's response.

Examples of the Practice of Dance Therapy
Psychiatry

Psychiatric Out-Patient Group

Eight young women, aged from 25 to 35, were referred for Dance by their psychotherapist. They were attending a weekly session of psychotherapy as a group, and this was preceded by an hour of Dance. It was a closed group, all members attending both sessions. All their diagnoses included some schizoid element. All had some degree of insight and no one demonstrated gross peculiarities in physical behaviour.

AIMS OF TREATMENT

Self awareness and self discovery, reinforcement of the psychotherapist's work.

Group awareness. Self in relation to the group.

Confidence in the supporting attitude of other members of the group.

Release of tension. Develop the ability to control emotions.

PROCEDURE

A "warm up" similar to that for a recreative group served to demonstrate superficial mood and underlying difficulties, enabling the therapist to adjust her programme and to lead the group into the dance, dance-drama, or improvisation which the group was working on.

Some of the difficulties demonstrated were that some people could not use the floor. They were unwilling to remove their shoes, or to sit or lie on it. Some could not expand into the horizontal plane of space. One could never make a direct movement as her whole body wobbled about and gestures were unclear. One was unable to grade her strength appropriately, making her seem more aggressive than she wanted to be. These difficulties usually reflected similar problems in the handling of life situations, for example, the girl who could never be direct, recognised her own weakness: she could not choose between one boyfriend and another, and let herself be pushed around by everyone.

All members worked together to help find ways of overcoming each other's problems in movement, and this never deteriorated into a 'talking shop'. They were active, co-operative and supportive of each other. Help was never rejected and self discovery was usually accompanied by laughter (led by the subject).

Set movement phrases or guided improvisation were used for mastering simple fundamental actions, such as curl up–open out–curl up again. This stresses awareness of the person's own centre and its relationship to the world. By adjusting the effort qualities in the phrase, suggesting that opening was done with strength and curling up with lightness, fine touch and sensitivity, the people found it easier and more satisfying as the strength had a purpose (overcoming their tendency to withdraw) and was balanced by its opposite.

Dance-dramas allowed for very wide interpretation. Movement characterisation, plot situations, and the pure movement of wind, water, sea, trees, etc., gave the therapist plenty of freedom to adapt themes to people's needs. The symbolism inherent in most dance and dance-drama material, eg. fairy stories, never adversely affected anyone, since situations were always resolved within the session. People chose their roles with surprisingly acute insight, and understood that choice of that role sometimes demonstrated that a 'sick' personality trait could be made to have a positive use.

RESULTS

The psychotherapist said that she found this group much easier to handle than other similar groups who did not dance together. The individuals were more accessible to treatment (psychotherapy) so her work progressed more rapidly than with former groups.

The group continued for about 10 months, when it became unnecessary as most people needed no further treatment. A Dance-Drama of the Pilgrim's Progress was the final piece of work, giving great opportunity for insight into the choice of characters. This was dressed and staged and performed to friends.

Long-Stay Psychiatric In-Patient Group

A group of ten chronic schizophrenic men who had been in hospital for 10 to 20 years were to be rehabilitated and placed out in the community. Part of their programme was to travel 40 minutes by bus to an old school hall and attend a Dance/Movement class held by two therapists. The project started with much help and support from the staff. This was gradually withdrawn so that patients took responsibility for themselves and travelled to the venue without prompting. Most of the group had no other treatment and no medication.

AIMS OF TREATMENT

To increase self confidence and responsibility.
To improve their communication skills.
To encourage initiative and decision-making.
To improve their physical competence.
To improve personal care, and social skills.

PROCEDURE

Sessions usually started with a 'tune-up' designed to prepare the body for action, and the mind for concentration, and to produce alertness and a happy mood. This developed into more specific movement experiences, including group, trio and partner relationships. Tasks were set which demanded inventiveness, leadership and 'give and take', and often a fairly robust 'dance' to music was devised.

RESULTS

Steady general improvement was observed in all members. Some people began to speak for the first time in years. They all moved more efficiently, walked without shuffling, and grotesque behaviour disappeared. They travelled to the venue individually sometimes arriving late after calling at a pub on the way, showing that they had developed some initiative!

During the 22 months that this project ran, all but one of the original group left, having gone to accommodation outside the hospital, too far away for them to continue coming.

Individually Treated Psychiatric In-Patient

G.B., an intelligent man in his twenties, diagnosed as schizophrenic, was referred for Movement. He was unsuitable for group work as he was argumentative, interfering and had a violent tic, which was a whole-body action and involved jumping, turning, flinging his arms about and pulling at his clothes.

AIMS OF TREATMENT

To reduce the tic.
To improve his behaviour towards others, by easing his frustration.

PROCEDURE

A variety of movement tasks were given, designed to discover how the tic started, and to find ways of avoiding or by-passing the initiating movement. Work was done on the merging of whole body movement into gesture, effort was introduced and transitions and variation of dynamics were taught. He could manage his body weight well enough to sway for a short time before the tic broke up the action. Spatial pathways were broken in the same way. He found it very difficult to make any movement which flowed from the centre to the periphery, and this made any resilient action almost impossible. A few dances were taught, to rather robust rhythmic music, eg. Lillibolero, or a Mazurka.

RESULTS
The patient became pleasanter, nicer to others, but as the tic had been established over many years, there was very little improvement in its control.

Patients Undergoing Psychotherapy

Patients undergoing depth analysis and psychotherapy have problems which are usually neurotic rather than psychotic. These problems include anxiety states, which may be due to some external threat that can neither be avoided nor eliminated, or to some internal conflict, showing in various inappropriate adaptations in behaviour and mental and/or physical symptoms.

The signs and symptoms may show in phobias, dissociation, regression, hysteria, insomnia, bad dreams, fantasies, emotional outbursts, withdrawal or intertia, also the inability to concentrate, and may also have somatic counterparts such as: headache, tachycardia, dyspnoea, anorexia or asthma and digestive disturbances. These conditions and the personality of the individual have to be taken into account continually, for it is necessary to consider the approach as treating an illness, rather than providing recreational activity, hoping it will be beneficial.

AIMS OF TREATMENT
The ultimate aim is wholeness, the ability to be centred, to 'stand on one's own feet', to relate to outward circumstances and people. A person can be guided, supported and encouraged, but eventually it is for him to be able to hold his own conflicts, and find his release. Healing comes from within. People often seem to want to be told what to do, to shelve responsibility, and expect the doctor or therapist to wave a

magic wand for the miracle drug to work or the burden to lift. The process of healing, however, often goes through painful periods, if there is to be an ultimate release. This is a different kind of suffering from that caused by illness, and those who can pursue it find eventually that it is infinitely worth while. This does not mean there is no enjoyment; there is an interchange in all stages.

It is possible for a person to go through life pursuing normal activities and yet have little body awareness, or sense of body image. By working towards such body awareness, paying attention to every part in isolation and co-ordination particularly in the effort qualities of the movement, inner participation develops, and mind, body and spirit begin to work together. People suffering from mental or psychological disturbance find they learn about their inner states through this experience of moving.

Those who find the dialectic process insufficient or too difficult need the involvement of the body to become whole human beings. Sportsmen and athletes, gymnasts and dancers recognise that they need a psychological as well as a physical approach in training in order to achieve and improve. Those who show their imbalance, reveal it in repetitive movement, neutralisation of effort, exaggeration of certain effort elements, lack or latency of elements or other movement irregularities, and then the psychic trauma has to be seriously considered.

PROCEDURE
Stance is very important for those who have little or no awareness of their centres; who are withdrawn; unable to face the world; who have weak egos; and no experience of the self, the upright within themselves. To be able to hold themselves with lifted chests and present themselves facing instead of presenting a shoulder, brings a sense of identity, 'I am' 'I can meet the world and communicate'. Working on planes, the centre, dimensions and strength are ways of approaching such difficulties.

Working on the floor has to be carefully undertaken as it can appear hostile to some; it suggests darkness, hardness, dirt, cold and entombment, but when people can allow themselves to contact the floor, rolling, resting, sitting, crawling, balancing, it becomes supportive, safe and secure. Then they can relax and from such an acceptable feeling, they come to find they can also use the floor to stamp, jump, somersault and run.

The depth at which movement can touch the unconscious must be constantly in mind. Though the same movement principles are used in psychotherapy as in physical training or treatment the aim is somewhat different. Where there is a problem in a healthy, balanced person it can be worked on directly; the approach in therapy needs to be indirect, a gradual disentangling process, before or interspersed with more definite, straightforward work, eg. in this connection skill in observation is essential, that is, being able to see in movement terms what a person is doing and how he does it at any given moment, without jumping to conclusions, or interpreting, except that the therapist can say to himself: "This looks as thought it might be ..." From watching in this way it is possible to make suggestions that the patient can utilise in his own way.

During the session one person was seen to be swaying slightly from one foot to the other. The therapist then said: "Do you see what you are doing?" "Can you increase the movement gradually?" "Can you take it round the room?" From this tiny start a variety of movement and active imagination arose. On another occasion, being in a drainpipe was mimed, and emergence was strong, flexible and slow, repeated until the drainpipe could be picked up and stood on one side, never to be used again. More than one person used this spontaneous idea, and each said it was like rebirth!

RESULTS

As people's movement vocabulary increases, and they become more at ease in their bodies, they experiment, and explore, not only the activity of moving and dancing, but what this is opening up in understanding, insight and deepening inner experience, and the form can sometimes be set as a dance. These few instances should show how important it is for the therapist/leader to become the observer/participator so that the mood, state or condition can be assessed and the next theme be decided on for further discovery.

Two Case Studies of Patients in Psychotherapy

These following case histories are examples of ways of working with patients, but they must not be regarded as patterns or formulae in treatment, for each patient's problems and potential should be individually assessed throughout the treatment period in order to adjust the programme appropriately. The two case histories have been chosen to show different ways of approach. Both were based on material the patients brought; one a repetitive movement, where flexibility was unusually predominant; the other a fantasy and a dream featuring respectively a spatial pattern and a dance.

Case 1 – Lena

Lena was an intelligent girl, who, though coming from a background with few advantages, nevertheless won her way to university by winning scholarships, but was not able to sustain the course. When referred to the therapist, the foregoing was the only information given by the analyst. Lena was again studying and achieved her degree during the time she was working with the therapist. This was some years ago, and having worked through her difficulties, she has subsequently lived a fulfilled life.

AIMS OF TREATMENT

As stated Lena was referred without any information or instructions, so the only guide was what was observed and her comments. The aim therefore was to develop her movement capacity, particularly the effort qualities that were latent, which led to her finding the solution to a long-standing problem, as related later.

PROCEDURE

At the first session she was asked to walk round the room in her normal manner; as she went she described and then performed the following repetitive movement – hands circling round each other, her whole body moving very flexibly, twisting and turning so that her feet made an equally twisted pattern on the floor. She felt it was significant, but didn't know how.

She could not use her hands alternately. She became able to do so by sitting on the floor, playing with hiding her hands and bringing them out first together and then separately. The hands were still curled up. Mime exercises and the idea of waves breaking as ripples and gradually becoming huge rollers, evoked the memory of a teacher who rapped her hands, and she could still sense the feel of the teacher's wedding ring.

Later this memory of the slapped hands recurred when she related how, at one centre she attended, she had been told she 'ought' to write like this, no wonder she couldn't stretch her fingers. Pushing, as though pushing away people led to her standing as though indicating: "This is my own space."

When moving forwards Lena was always drawing back in the centre of her body. Bending her legs and going down towards the floor, keeping the body erect; using a hand to draw her forwards, and moving with hands clasped behind her back, were ways that helped her to be aware of her centre. Unravelling an imaginary tangle of threads, she was soon using her hands alternately, in wide movements, narrowing close to her body and then spreading again, involving her centre.

Always on her toes, Lena found jumping difficult. When she asked to work on feet, she came by degrees to use the soles in contact with the floor, and using her heels, and by transferring her weight to the different parts of her feet, she found she could use her energy to jump.

So far the therapist worked from the movement observed, then Lena began to talk about herself. Men had such an effect on her that she was unable to resist anything they wanted, and some people made her feel 'sick' and in a 'muddy whirlpool'. Her mother was one; she would fly into rages and get attention by becoming ill. Lena wanted to find her own standpoint.

The original repetitive movement was introduced at times as respite from smooth gliding movements. It became known as her 'whirlpool'. At the fifth session in six weeks, she was given two options, and chose to dance her 'whirlpool', and seek to change to straighter movement; the therapist noticed her one day moving her arms alternately, with sweeping gestures, stepping in the same way and really enjoying it. The suggestion was then given that she create a dance starting with the 'whirlpool', feeling as though she were being swirled along by wind and water, then to see if she could find a firm rock under her feet. The therapist improvised on the piano, when suddenly

Lena stood stock still, drew herself up and said: "That's the first time I've been able to discriminate."

Only years later when asked whether she would allow her material to be published did she write: "It had made all the difference to all sorts of things. I'd been plugging away at discrimination for ages in my analysis, so it was one of your successes." A great deal of work was done on the dance, setting it and the music, and eventually she danced to her analyst and his wife, also an analyst.

RESULT

From this time Lena talked more about herself, and worked for quite a long time further, dealing with difficult situations, sorting out relationships, and she coped without falling into a depression when her mother finally became bedridden. It wasn't till quite near the end of working with the therapist that, having previously found the floor inimical, she was able to say: "That's the first time I've wanted to go down" and was then really able to work on the floor, kneeling, rising and sinking, rolling and moving about on it.

Case 2 – Pamela

Pamela was secretary to an M.P. and working with an analyst who referred her for dance therapy, because she had had two dreams, one in which she was dancing, the other developed into an obsessive fantasy as described below.

PROCEDURE

At her first session, Pamela related this fantasy based on a drama. The fantasy was an S within a circle in which she was caught up and whirled around; she could neither get out nor anyone else get in. Her dream was an ogress mother with an enormous head, a huge swollen foot and no body. Pamela, as the daughter, was not crushed by the mother but dancing in front of her.

For Pamela, the aim was to find release from her obsessional fantasy, to develop a better balance between the opposites of her personality and to make relationships.

Programme: The pattern of the S in the circle indicated working on space (area). The reason for this was that Pamela was intellectually orientated, and Laban equated the 4 qualities of movement with Jung's 4 functions of the psyche.

Motion Factors	Functions
Weight (energy, force)	Sensation
Space	Intellect (thinking)
Time	Intuition
Flow	Feeling (evaluation)

The suggested movements were the exploration of zones of space by each limb in turn. Pamela drew the shape of a cone, the apex at the shoulder of the arm, or the hip for the leg, within the cone shape bending, stretching and twisting, also involving the motion factors. She drew a circle with her right foot on the floor, and then a figure 8. Later her attention was drawn to the fact that she had separated the circle, and the figure 8 could be seen as being formed of two S's intersecting at the centre.

Pamela wrote: "I feel I must say how terribly grateful I am for our effort on Saturday. You really were brilliant with your figure 8. My analyst is delighted."

Sequences were created using the figure 8 a number of times. Piano accompaniment was improvised, so the sequences became nearly dance-like. A pastel drawing was brought showing a large figure 8 lying horizontally, and below it the ogress within the pattern of the circle and the S inside. Noticing a slight break where the S touched the circle the therapist said: "If that were a piece of string, you could take the end and whip it out into a straight line. A model was produced by Pamela of a woman in a figure 8 but no circle, holding a pen.

From working on space (area) Pamela progressed to effort elements: particularly she worked on strength and lightness and directness and flexibility in order to bring together thinking and sensation. Moving with her chest lifted helped her to gain lightness.

A third dream was of a woman walking with a star on her chest, and a light throwing her shadow in front. The shadow idea was worked on by electric light, but doing this on her own, Pamela found the shadow was not only thrown on the floor, but on the walls increasing in size, causing terror. Luckily she realised it was dangerous to continue alone.

A fourth dream followed the shadow. She was fighting with a woman. To start with they had equal strength until Pamela

kicked the other downstairs. The therapist received no information from the analyst, so did not know that Pamela was
considered to live her 'shadow' side, but was aware of the
significance of the shadow.

Pamela produced a final painting of a woman in a figure 8
holding a star, and in the sky was a red star in a circle in a dark
background.

RESULT
Several more sessions consolidated this work. The fantasy
disappeared and was replaced by the constructive use of the
intellect in writing books.

Eating Disorders

Treatment by Naomi Milen, B.A. Dance, B.A. Psychology,
working at Atkinson Morley's and Middlesex Hospitals in
London.

For brevity, these notes are limited to group treatment of
anorexic women in hospital.

These patients often have an obsessive tendency to use
energetic or violent exercise to "burn off calories" and this is
contra-indicated when weight-gain and acceptance of a bigger
body is the aim of treatment, and often of immediate importance
to life. The patients see their bodies as something loathsome,
and their movement experience as an undifferentiated 'blob'.
Distorted ideas of body image prevent reasoning and argument,
despite comparison of their own bodies with that of a healthy
person. They tend to be egocentric and withdrawn and the
symbolism of eating extends into the 'give and take' of other
activities of living. The distorted body image is shown in
drawings, eg. no limbs, separation or huge size of certain body
parts, such as breasts and thighs, or a body without feet.

AIMS OF TREATMENT
To introduce the idea that their bodies need not be
antagonistic – "We are working with, not against, ourselves,
rather than taking a dance training."

To present points of reference for the anorexic to experience her body in; to cope with her size as she gains weight and
to help her towards a better sense of reality.

WORKING PRINCIPLE

The work and structure presented can be cathartic, but it goes beyond catharsis in re-integrating the fractured being. The importance and function of both processes of separating and piecing together cannot be over-emphasised. Insight into separate elements of their illness eventually generates a much stronger sense of "whole self". Grounding and centering work can help the individual to find his/her strength. The concept of strength is significant for the anorexic. In dance, it can be found as a positive energy. It can be enjoyed even in delicate and lighter movements and in stillness. The ability to feel rooted without being weighted down by size; of feeling powerful without feeling destructive, is exciting and fulfilling for the anorexic, as it gives her control, other than through the use of food alone. Pelvic action is very important. The pelvis often feels 'dead' or 'loaded', and for many of these women, it is a relief to move this area specifically, in a non-threatening experience; or even as a playful anatomy lesson. The dance therapist must be prepared to handle various emotions as they surface, either verbally or through dance, and to decide whether the group should help or share these.

WORKING EXAMPLE

A group of six or seven women, aged between 18 and 40, who had spent between 3 and 4 months in hospital. They all suffered from eating disorders and distorted body image. The dance sessions lasted about two hours each.

In this positively committed group, it was possible to undertake an exploration of movement and its therapeutic and healing potentials. Their own unique and authentic movement was encouraged – not a performance to 'please the teacher'. A safe environment was provided to enable all kinds of exploration. For many people, the body in motion is a most vulnerable and exposing process, so in these sessions the emphasis was on creating as non-competitive a feeling as possible. Time was given to encouraging and awakening, and to encountering the aliveness within, so that they could feel the difference from the manic hyperkinaesis familiar to them. For some, it was a chance to admit to the tiredness or weakness they actually may have been feeling, allowing them to submit gently to this in movement. Some were helped to discover that a creative process did exist for them, measured not by how much is produced, but by the experience of a qualitative state; the quiet finding and unfolding of an image. Creativity helped towards identifying the self. They found a quality of energy or imagination through the body that was not self-negating, nor wholly concerned with shape or appearance. The process always alleviated some measure of anxiety. Relaxation techniques were also used.

RESULTS

These patients showed an improvement in accepting their bodies as part of their whole self. They became more aware of the group and began to trust others. They became better able to nourish themselves physically, and they also began to ingest and digest feelings, movements and aspects of their body/mind selves, without such punishing measures as starvation and purgation.

As there is such emphasis on process rather than goal in this work, a new image of what is possible with one's body can be built, and movement becomes a life-enhancing element.

These patients also had the following treatments:- psychotherapy, behaviour modification, and occupational therapy, including other arts.

Psycho-Geriatric Patients

Work done by Sister Iris Turner, R.M.N., at Herne Hospital, Kent.

The patients were groups of confused, elderly women, all chair-bound due to various causes, including strokes and arthritis. They were withdrawn and self-centred.

AIMS OF TREATMENT

To increase the range of movement in the whole body.
Orientation towards reality.
Communication through movement.
To increase confidence and self-value.
To improve ability to be creative and to make choices.

To give pleasure and enjoyment.
To improve relationships with staff and others in the group.

PROCEDURE
The working principles were based on Laban's movement analysis. Dramatic themes were used, based on events from the earlier lives of group members, aided by music. 'Props' were used to encourage the movements the patients needed. Dance and mime ideas developed as the work progressed. Sessions usually lasted half an hour, and were extended if needed. Sometimes, they were planned for a particular patient; sometimes for the whole group.

RESULTS
There was reported a generally improved and happier atmosphere in the ward. The patients' movement improved so that they were able to do small things for themselves, and thus increase their confidence and self-value. Patients were more alert and sat upright in their chairs, looking outwards. Sometimes they volunteered information about their past lives. They also began to talk to each other.

Physical Applications

Brain Damage (Strokes-CVA)
Although more research is needed, it seems that dance, based on movement analysis, can be a help to a patient with hemiplegia due to a C.V.A.

AIMS OF TREATMENT
The aims vary for each patient according to the area of damage and the problems encountered by the patient, but dance can be used to help in the following ways:
Co-ordination in practical tasks.
The finer co-ordination of Effort/Shape needed for non-verbal communication.

To improve orientation in space.

Overcoming depression, frustration and loss of confidence, since dance is a creative and adaptable medium and can be adjusted to meet a wide variety of needs.

Functional tasks clearly demonstrate success or failure, but the patient's need to achieve is very great. This can be satisfied in dance where, within the limits of the 'anti-spasm' pattern, there is no right or wrong, only difference or variety, and the dance can be tailored to the patient's potential. This work should be based on Bobath and the pattern of spasm understood. Vigilant monitoring is needed with creative work as the patient is allowed some choice of movement. He will be asked to attempt tasks and respond to challenges. This is intended to develop consciously controlled, purposeful movements, while at the same time retraining the unconscious supporting mechanisms.

Co-ordination depends on appropriate Effort/Shape variations, and these can be explained and taught by using the unaffected side first. Therapists often convey a feeling for the required effort qualities and variations by the way they handle the patient. Difficulties in creating these dynamics can impair emotional expression and thus cause frustration.

Combating a disability is a praiseworthy approach, but the attitudes of fighting weight with force usually increases spasm. If the patient can experience changes in effort qualities and learn to produce them himself, then he can deliberately reduce the tension or force and increase the lightness or fine touch as he feels the resistance of spastic muscles inhibiting his action. In other words, he learns to combat resistance, not with a fighting quality, but with sensitivity and lightness, which is an unfamiliar idea, especially for men. This could prove a profitable field for further research.

Functional actions do not only have a pathway in space but phrasing and rhythm as well. This is dependent on effort variations dictated by the desired action (eg. rising from a chair) and modified by the patient's proportions and personality. The best rhythm for a particular patient needs to be found and he will then have to feel it and remember it. Singing or other vocal sounds can help to convey the right dynamics and help the patient to form a concept of the action phrase he intends to do.

This movement imagination, movement memory, or concept is often lost as a result of C.V.A. and the patient can be compared with a gymnast attempting a difficult new movement which she has never seen or thought of before. A rhythmic phrase has to be created, with a starting position, climax and finishing position and use of body parts in a spatial pathway and in relation to each other. Sometimes, the action can be broken down into shorter or easier phrases and practised as dance, before the functional task is tackled.

For example: throwing a ball requires that more than one effort quality is changed at the same time. Even if the patient can take his arm through the spatial pathway and open the hand, the ball often falls at his feet, because he cannot also increase his strength, aim and speed all at the moment when he has to open the hand. In dance, these increases can be learnt separately, and graded, so that all three effort elements do not have to be varied at the same time until more mastery is acquired.

Consider space and balance in the hemiplegic patient. The idea or feeling of the high – deep dimension seems to be lost, broken or misplaced to the side. The patient has lost his centre; even the concept of a centre. Hence the connection between head and feet is disturbed. The relationship between upper and lower body has to be re-established. Without a centre, it is very difficult to feel the relationship between opposite hand and foot. It is difficult to reach out into space without a centre through which stability is integrated. If these actions are achieved, it is often without inner participation, because the centre is not involved and strategies have been invented.

For example: opening and closing in the horizontal plane, even in very small movements, compatible with symmetry, helps to establish the vertical axis and bilaterality. Contracting and expanding in the sagital plane, though difficult, helps to regain the centre, and is a preparation for the many body management actions such as getting into a car, or standing upright.

PROCEDURE

This work is best preceded by physiotherapy and neuro facilitation. Dance ideas can be used to stimulate all the sitting and floor exercises and later, the standing ones.

Working with a partner, and in a group, allows resting time and encourages people to learn to check on their own movements. Partnership also provides a change in the roles of helper and helped. Reaching, turning or rolling towards a partner; stepping patterns, such as circles, squares, triangles, or someone's initials; stepping forwards, backwards, sideways and diagonally can all be dancelike; and eg. diagonal and crossed steps lead naturally into a tango!

Conventional dances such as the Can-Can or Hornpipe can be done sitting if necessary, but very great care is needed if music is used because it is usually too fast; people will want to keep with it, especially if it has a firm beat, and attempting this will increase spasm and the movement will deteriorate. It is far better to sing, unless the therapist can play an instrument.

Examples of creative ideas and tasks:
- Where can you reach with your heel?
- Invent a sequence of three places to reach to.
- Try to reach across to the other side.
- Show your sequence to a partner to copy.
- Make each reach bigger than the last.
- Bring in a slow part and then some quick bits – make a rhythmic sequence out of this.
- Bring hands to meet – palms meeting – backs meeting – edges meeting etc. Invent a sequence – do it with a partner.
- Make round, flat or spiky shapes with the hands. Carve shapes in the air. Do this with elbows or knees, and if sitting, with the feet. Various leg gestures, done sitting or standing, are common in dances and help to stabilise the hips.

Improvisation of this sort can be done to music, with the cautions mentioned above. Often it is better to use music which does not have a very clear rhythmic beat but creates feeling or atmosphere.

This type of work needs peace and quiet, a chance to concentrate, and a feeling of open-ended time to achieve one's aims. The people need to work in a separate room away from onlookers, noise and other distractions.

Case History of a Stroke Patient

Mrs. X., a woman of 75, suffered a C.V.A. Physiotherapy was followed by occupational therapy, which started 4 months later.

The patient had a right hemiplegia, dysphasia and dyspraxia, but could walk alone without a stick, though the right foot dragged and the right hip showed spastic internal rotation. There was some circumduction of leg and no contrary arm swing. The right hand had very poor grip, no supination, and the fingers could not move separately. The patient rejected the affected limbs. Mrs. X had been very active, with many interests and no previous impairment of movement.

AIMS OF TREATMENT

To improve all movement, walking, use of both hands together, finer movements of the right hand. Psychologically: to lift the depression, help reduce tension (the patient had high blood pressure), and to encourage verbal ability. Loneliness and boredom had to be coped with.

Though suffering from the acute exhaustion common in stroke patients, Mrs. X. hid her depression and worked hard. Being intelligent, artistic and musical, dance became an important part of her O.T. activities. She was treated for 2 hours once a week. Treatment was based on Bobath and developed through the Laban principles of movement outlined above.

PROCEDURE

As the patient was observed arriving, walking down the road, the therapist could assess fatigue, co-ordination, balance and psychological state, and adjust her plan accordingly. Dance treatment included movements stressing relationship of body parts with the whole, limbs with each other, exploring their zones, meeting across the mid-line. Particular attention was paid to the play of hands with each other, clapping at many different places around the body. Relationship of head to shoulders, and shoulder to hips and the way a body part can lead a movement, or the movement can be initiated in the body centre, helped the patient with her dyspraxia, and minimised rejection of right side.

Variations of Effort were introduced and explained and demonstrated in simple ball games, and contact with the therapist. This was to help the performance of functional and expressive tasks, and regain the rhythmic phrasing of dynamics needed for normal movement.

Awareness of effort variations was heightened by games based on hand-clasps, the patient reproducing with the sound side the exact effort variations in the therapist's handclasp of the affected hand. This was reversed and developed to give the patient the opportunity to create her own choices and convey them or express them as a hand dance. Effort variations required for walking or rising from a chair were experienced, sometimes with music, in a dance or play situation (see examples).

Space work on the kinaesphere helped her to develop a symmetry and laterality, to establish her centre, and to experience non-spastic movements in the context of whole body opening and closing. Improvisational work requires careful monitoring to avoid the typical patterns of hemiplegia, but as Mrs. X. understood the aims this was possible.

Examples of Dances used in Mrs. X's Treatment Sessions

MIMETIC DANCE
Tight-rope artiste for stable balance and placing the feet in line.
Clown on a tight rope for labile balance, adjustment of knees and feet.
Strap-hanging in a train, for labile balance and resilient knees.
Ski-ing for whole body shaping, feet together, weight on heels, springy knees. Hips working against shoulders.

DANCE
Hornpipe, use of heel with extended leg. Hands working together.
Brahms Waltz, crossing the mid-line, turning around the sound side, cross stepping, big arm movements.
Tango, cross stepping, leading the movement with shoulders or hips.

IMPROVISATIONS
Various swinging dances to waltzes.
Field's "Rondo" – tossing imaginary bubbles about all over the place, requiring balance, quickness, lightness, use of head and eyes, and initiative in finding new places to move to. Good antidote to depression.
Making shapes with the hands – rounded, flat, spiky shapes; one hand copying the other or complementing it; enfolding it or escaping from it, or moving in response to the therapist's hand.
Making whole body shapes; relating opposite arms and legs; leg

gestures (ie. non-weight-bearing actions of the legs) to improve stability around the hip.

RESULTS

After 6 months Mrs. X.'s balance and walking were greatly improved. Contrary movement of arms was beginning, and whole body movements such as rising from the floor were mastered. Drawing and writing with the right hand were possible though difficult.

At 9 months, as more attention was paid to the artistic and creative side of dance, she became more cheerful, could walk on uneven surfaces, and with a springy gait, and most functional skills were adequate to her needs except hand sewing. She enjoyed inventing her own dances to music at home and bringing them to the O.T. sessions. She was making fairly good effort variations, and flow changes and could manage her body quite well; she could play bowls, often accurately, from half the normal distance.

Mrs. X. became slightly more talkative. It was observed that work involving hand holds seemed to help the dysphasia, and the therapist used a warm handclasp when the patient was unable to find a word. This sometimes worked suprisingly well, but not always. No reason for this is suggested.

Note – this patient also had one or two hours a week of more conventional occupational therapy activities including shopping, painting, carpentry (D.I.Y.) and other ambidextrous tasks, all requiring movement. Problems encountered in these jobs were often analysed and tackled in a dance experience or with a percussion instrument. Movement study integrated the O.T. programme.

Working in Holloway Prison

Work done by Flick Long B.Ed., M.A. (trained at University of London, Goldsmiths' College).

Holloway is a large women's prison in London. Ms. Ling has worked in a unit where she was in charge of a team of five specialists treating about 30 women on a daily basis. Using their skills flexibly, the team incorporate personal care, counselling and social education within and amongst the activities of dance, painting, music, drama and craft. The age range is 16 to 80 years. Typical diagnoses are personality disorder, depression, psychopathy, schizophrenia. Admittance to psychiatric hospitals is often not possible because of the violence of the women's behaviour. They have often both suffered and inflicted assault and cruelty, their crimes including arson and murder. Often disturbing in appearance, they are the outcasts of society and are likely to be suspicious, unpredictable and aggressive.

AIMS OF TREATMENT
Communication to establish relationship and trust. Expression contained within the discipline of an art form. Establishment of worth and identity ie. a good self image. Recognition of potential for life and acceptability within society.

THEORY
This has a basis in the movement principles of Laban and is not strictly limited to dance.

"The key is to see each patient as a unique individual with his own range of movement energy and form of expression. Each person organises this energy differently."[1]

"Dance as a physical therapeutic tool seems to be particularly relevant for such disturbed women (in Holloway) ... Thus it seems appropriate to work back through physical expression and begin to place it in an ordered form."[2]

Flick Ling is actively involved in developing the theory of movement-dance therapy and trying to establish her own working ideas. In practice she emphasises above all the need for the therapist to be genuinely caring, vividly and flexibly involved in the immediate practical situation.

PROCEDURE
Information about medical and prison background through case conferences and discussion provides a basis for assessing individual needs and consequent treatment.

Although substantial general thought and preparation is

1. "Dance Therapy" in *Visual Encyclopedia of Unconventional Medicine* ed. A. Hill, New English Library, 1979.
2. In Touch in Prison Service Journal No. 51. 1983.

needed, sessions are not planned in detail. The structure has to be loose because mood and behaviour are unpredictable and the group size and constitution uncertain.

Since the heightened expression of dance may be threatening, work usually begins with a controlled warm-up physically and emotionally. The crucial content of a session might for example be practical participation, social and artistic, in achieving a group performance. Or the work might be more individual and symbolic. Finally there is an emphasis on group awareness and an adjustment towards re-entry into everyday prison life.

Within the plan the practice may recognise the importance of:

Body Imagery. This (the mental picture of the body which underpins the bodily ego and, in turn, the self-concept) may be pivotal to the power of individual work.

Non-Verbal Communication. Through the movements of non-verbal communication (perhaps the most authentic expression) both the recognition of problems and a restoration of the ability to relate may be possible.

RESULTS

Most obviously the women begin to smile and respond positively to others and to appreciate rather than mutilate their own bodies. Movement which is puppet-like or disorganised becomes more coherent and acceptable, integrating feeling and behaviour. There is less violence, anger and fear and a genuine interest begins in achieving something artistic which goes beyond self-concern. The specific value of such work in a prison environment also extends beyond the confines of the unit.

Paediatric Applications

Autism

There are varying schools of thought as to the causes of autism, some maintaining it is organic, others psychological and environmental, whereas mental handicap means a state of arrested or incomplete development of mind resulting from many causes.

AIMS OF TREATMENT
The main aim with the autistic person is to make a relationship, to stimulate response to, communication with and trust of another person, then people in general.

PROCEDURE
Body contact: rocking, rolling, balancing, climbing on or over.
Moving: in, around or to and from one or more people.
Sound: humming, singing, making noises, percussion, variations in speed, time, rhythm and volume, stimulating or accompanying movement.
Music: improvisation, playing to, playing with, learning to listen.

In using these approaches, the aim of dance should not be forgotten, therefore, however serious the actual treatment, it should be undertaken with playfulness, encouragement and sensitivity, in order that there may be enjoyment and fun as a preliminary to the lightheartedness that may be experienced in dance. When children can accept certain interference and restriction by learning and not to react negatively to frustration and definite refusal, they can begin to co-operate and enter into a relationship with one other person, and then gradually more than one person.

EXAMPLES
1. A horizontal ladder on a climbing frame is useful. A child can be on the frame and an adult put a hand on the rung immediately in front of him, but at the first hint of annoyance, move to the next rung; gradually it can turn into a game, when the child lifts the hand and places it on the next rung.

2. A child may expect to be able to do the same thing to each helper. For instance, having climbed on one person's back, he may think he can do that with everyone and be mystified, if not upset, by refusal. Children can be very persistent. One boy tried three times to do this and eventually the therapist picked him up and to his astonishment put him on his back on the floor, but immediately played with him. At the penultimate session he tried again; when she surprised him creeping up behind her with

a wicked grin, she grinned and laughed and shook her finger at him saying "No, not on my back," and he promptly hugged her.

When such a relationship can be established, then joining in with others can be attempted, such as holding out a hand to invite a child to come into a circle and participate of his own volition, rather than being just taken by the hand and led into a circle. Treated in this way the children are not resistant, and the circle can gain a much more dance-like quality.

RESULTS

Following the application of the above techniques, an evaluation was made. Statistically the results were not very promising. However these had been collated from the tapes of one video camera only, and assessed quantitatively not qualitatively. In particular the senior staff maintained that clinically results had been obtained, and the group, several of whom were members of staff who had worked on the project with the children, agreed. Especially in the film that was made, it was plain that some of the children's faces gradually changed from expressions of deep anxiety to joy and pleasure, and all developed a readiness to work not only with the adults, but with each other. The sound they made was chaotic at the start, but became quieter and more harmonious, until it was possible to introduce music.

The leader visited the group several times some months later, and on one occasion a little girl, finding herself alone at one end of the gym, came right across to where the leader was sitting, sat down beside her and cuddled up against her. Another day the teenage boy of the 'wicked grin' was coming down an outside staircase with head bent, and as she passed, he looked up, and seeing her, a shy smile lit up his face, like any normal child.

Asthmatic Children

The following two cases are an example of how the same symptoms had to be treated quite differently: the boy (case 1) having to be allowed to experience the material from his own unconscious, and to find his own way of dealing with it in the security of the therapeutic session; the girl (case 2) being satisfactorily treated in a group.

Case 1 – Michael

Michael was eleven when he came for movement. He had suffered very badly with asthma and always had his atomiser handy, though at times he did without it altogether. He was a very intelligent boy, with a bent toward science, particularly astronomy.

PROCEDURE

Michael was very limp at the start and could not stand more than 30 minutes work, though he did manage the full hour later. First, he found a yellow ball and dribbled it and rolled it against the walls. He used percussion very quietly, and played with a tiny top. He made all sorts of shapes with small equipment. All this play seemed to fulfil a basic need.

AIMS OF TREATMENT

Exercises were introduced next, to help his tight hamstrings and to expand his chest, eg. floor work:-
Prone. Reaching back with hands, catching feet and rocking, to extend the thoracic spine and expand the chest.
Supine. Moving around, balancing on different parts of the body, particularly shoulders and feet. This also helped the chest expansion. Interspersed with such work on the body, the therapist introduced the idea that he should act something. Starting with a slashing movement, he developed this into fencing, and then into fighting with a sword.
Examples of other mimed ideas:-
a) One series started by his being swallowed by an octopus; he was wearing a space suit and therefore was safe inside the octopus in a storm. Eventually he cut his way out. To bring the series to an end, he undid his oxygen mask and drowned. The therapist suggested that a part of him had died and a part was still alive. This led to a judgement, his punishment being to run 58 miles in hell, covering himself with sand to protect himself from hell's flames. In the end he earned himself a ticket to leave and go to heaven.
b) A kapok mattress was produced, which he attacked as representing two people with whom he was angry.
c) There were many struggles with a monster in the sea and on land, and with a lion.
d) Sometimes he and the therapist listened together to a

drama workshop on the radio, and Michael used some of the ideas.

In the end he came in one day saying "I'm tired of monsters and octopusses". The Therapist was aware of the significance of all this activity but made no attempt to interpret it. She let him work things out in his actions.

RESULTS

Soon after starting the drama work, he asked to be in a school play, and though he used to move as in a mist of sleep, he became strong and dynamic when he had the experience of struggling with the monsters, etc.

He had had difficulty in mixing, but this seemed to be overcome by the time he arrived at university, where he seems to have become the centre of a group and goes on enterprising expeditions. He appears to have grown out of the anxiety caused by the asthma, and the fear of being rushed into hospital during an attack.

He had worked with this therapist for two years.

Case 2 – Holly

Aged about seven, attending Primary School and suffering from asthma, Holly joined a small recreational dance class run by one of the authors. Her doctor asked that every opportunity be taken to help the child's chest expansion.

PROCEDURE

Themes suitable for all the children were introduced, and as guidance was given to each child according to her needs, Holly was treated without being singled out.

Example:- All the children were asked to fly round the room, flinging their arms out and bending back, to Khachaturian's Masquerade Waltz. Each child was free to find her own way of responding, but in all cases the task demanded expansion of the chest.

Once in each session Holly was asked to lie supine on a box and slide herself along till her shoulders dropped over the edge, when the therapist caught her. Sometimes the same type of opening out action was done sitting on the therapist's lap and dropping back over her knees.

As well as body training, the children created their own

dances and movement sequences. Holly was very inventive; she and her younger sister, who joined the group when old enough, had a wealth of imaginative ideas. Together they worked out some most interesting movement patterns, body shaping and qualities.

The therapist made no mention of asthma, the chest, nor of breathing. The sessions were recreational and for enjoyment, and the fact that Holly did not consciously have to do set exercises was no doubt an advantage.

This is an example of how it is possible to treat an individual specifically, within a group. Concentration and attention were on the group dance or movement, and not focussed on remedial exercises which would have reminded the patient of her disability, and would have caused tension and rigidity. She was dancing with pleasure as a member of a group.

Results

The asthma disappeared completely. The doctor who examined her at her secondary school, surprised to hear that she had ever had asthma, attributed her recovery to Laban Movement and Dance. This was the only new activity she had done.

Multiply Handicapped Adults

Work done by Janette Allan-Jones at Ravenswood Village, Berks.

The patients are a small group of severely brain-damaged, grossly mentally handicapped, wheelchair-bound adults in their twenties. Two are blind, only one can speak. Most have cerebral palsy, with spasm and/or tremor, plus other neurological disease, one of which is progressive. Unassisted, there is very little movement possible, except rolling, opening the hand, or lifting the head or arm. There is poor motivation, difficulty in communication and comprehension, and a tendency to withdrawal. Movement of the body is not a total experience.

AIMS OF TREATMENT

To facilitate as much movement exploration as bodies will allow.

To give individual body awareness.

To increase spatial awareness.

To develop a movement vocabulary.

To develop relationships and communication through movement.

To improve self-confidence and stimulate interest in the world around through sound and touch as well as proprioception and the other senses.

To facilitate education.

PROCEDURE

Laban-based working principles are used (see General Theory section). A variety of techniques are used to encourage movement, eg. games, simple songs, percussion, rhymes etc. All work is done on a one-to-one basis within the group. Movement dance work done in these sessions is always relevant to daily living eg. reaching out for a biscuit at break time, balancing on the lavatory, movements to assist dressing.

Note – Within the limits of this group, this may be included as dance, as it fulfils the definition of dance.

RESULTS

Attention span increased, and awareness extended beyond the wheelchair.

Rigidity and spasm were reduced, and patients became more relaxed.

Relationships became easier.

Self-expression became easier.

Some words were given a meaning through movement.

Visually Handicapped Adults

Work done by Christine Erne Dip.C.O.T. in Haringey, London.

The clients were of both sexes and had recently lost most of their sight.

AIMS OF TREATMENT
To give confidence in moving freely around their environment.
To improve breathing and posture.
To heighten body awareness and spatial awareness.
To provide a social activity.

PROCEDURE
Relaxation techniques were used initially. Sometimes partners helped and supported each other as they moved. A large space was available, giving the freedom to move unhindered. Technical teaching offered precision and structure. The planes and dimensions were stressed to relate the kinaesphere to general space.

RESULTS
The clients seem less rigid. They are able to move more freely. They are more relaxed, and though 'free' movement causes them some inhibition, they are gradually improving in this too.
The clients can find their way about a room more easily and with more confidence. Social dance, eg. square dancing, is enjoyed without any timidity.

Useful Information

TRAINING
In the United Kingdom so far there is no recognised training nor qualification in Dance Therapy. To work in this field, people have to put together a package of training for themselves, usually limited to dance and psychology, which narrows their field accordingly. However, those health care professionals who are interested could benefit from the following courses:-
1. The Association for Dance-Movement Therapy.

One or two-day introductory courses in a wide variety of techniques.

2. The Laban Centre.

Courses in Dance. And courses for teachers of children with special needs.

The Laban Centre now offers a postgraduate M.A. degree course in Dance Therapy. The degree is validated by an American university (Hahnemann University).

3. Laban International Courses.

A summer holiday course annually, and other short courses. There is usually some aspect relevant to therapeutic work. Students may make a progressive study carrying on over 4 to 6 years.

4. University of Surrey.

A new B.A.(Hons.) course called "Dance in Society". This course offers, among other special studies, an option on "Dance Therapy". It is not clear yet whether graduates would be considered professional therapists.

5. Laban Movement Workshops for Therapists.

A new organisation offering studies in the application of movement to the treatment of physical and psychological illness/handicap, for people already working in the therapeutic field. Its address: Bonnyes, Hadley Common, Herts. EN5 5QG. U.K.

Other addresses can be found under addresses such as the American Dance Therapy Association and The Laban-Bartenieff Institutute for Movement Study. These two American organisations can advise on training in the U.S.A., where several universities offer degree courses in Dance Therapy.

Bibliography

Bainbridge, Collingdon, Duddington & Gardner, "Dance-Mime, a contribution to treatment in Psychiatry", *Journal of Mental Science*, Vol. XCIX, No. 415, April 1953.

Bartenieff, I., *Body Movement, Coping with the Environment*, Gordon & Breach.

Howlett, M & H. "Dance, Theory and Practice", available from authors; Department Teacher Training, Birmingham Polytechnic.

Laban, R., *A Life for Dance*, Macdonald & Evans.

Laban & Lawrence, *Effort*, Macdonald & Evans.

Laban & Ullman, *Modern Educational Dance*, Macdonald & Evans.

Laban Guild Magazines. Nos. 6, 9, 10, 11, 16, 20, 21, 27, 34, 36, 55, 62, 65, 70 (Notation), 71 (Notation).

Lefco, H., *Dance Therapy*, Nelson Hall, Chicago, 1974.

Ling, F., "In Touch", *Prison Service Journal*, No. 51, New Series, July 1983

Lowen, A., *The Betrayal of the Body*, Collier Macmillan.

Preston-Dunlop, V., *Practical Kinetography Laban*, Macdonald & Evans.

Russell, J., *Creative Dance in the Primary School*, Macdonald & Evans.

Sherbourne, V., *Creative Therapy*, S. Jennings (ed), Chapter – Movement for Retarded and Disturbed Children, Kemble Press, 1983.

Sherbourne, V., *Physical & Creative Activities for the Mentally Handicapped*, G. Upton (ed). Three Chapters: 1. The Significance of Early Movement Experiences in the development of severely retarded children. 2. Content of developmental movement programme. 3. Physical Education Programme in a Special School.

Sherbourne, V., *Physical Education for Special Needs*, Ed. L. Groves, Cambridge University Press. Chapter – Movement for developmentally retarded children.

Veronica Sherbourne has made four films available from Concorde Films, Felixstowe Road, Ipswich, Suffolk.

A fifth film, Building Bridges, is available from New York University Library.

Thornton, S., *A Movement Perspective of Rudolf Laban*, Macdonald & Evans.

Turner, I. "The Use of Drama and Movement Therapy with Elderly Confused Patients". Available from author, 27 Stourton View, Frome, Somerset, or c/o "Sesame", address below.

Wethered, A., *Drama and Movement in Therapy*, Macdonald & Evans.

Addresses

The American Dance Therapy Association,
Suite 210, 1000 Century Plaza, Columbia, Maryland 21044, U.S.A.

The Association for Dance-Movement Therapy,
99 South Hill Park, London NW3 2SP.

Bundesverband für Tanztherapie,
Monheim, Marienburg (3 yr. training, details from Laban Centre).

Central Council for Physical Recreation,
Francis House, Francis Street, London, S.W.1.

Centre for Personal Construct Psychology,
132 Warwick Way, London SW1V 4JD.

Chantraine School of Dance,
47 Compayne Gardens, London NW6 3DB.

Concord Films Ltd. (films by Sherbourne can be hired).
Nacton, Ipswich, Suffolk, IP10 0JZ.

Disabled Living Foundation,
380-384 Harrow Road, London W9 2HU.

The Laban Centre,
Laurie Grove, London, SE14 5NW.

The Laban Guild,
Picket Hill House, Picket Hill, Ringwood, Hants.

The Laban-Bartenieff Institute for Movement Study,
133 W.21 St., New York, NY 10011, U.S.A. (American Titles).

Laban International Courses,
c/o Ivy Cottage, Clockhouse Lane, Egham, Surrey.

Language of Dance Centre,
17 Holland Park, London W11 3TD.

Perls Institute. Germany (details from Laban Centre).

Scottish Committee for Art and Disability,
18-19 Claremont Crescent, Edinburgh EH7 4QD.

Sesame (Mainly Drama and Movement),
Christchurch, 27 Blackfriars Road, London S.E.1.

Shape, 9 Fitzroy Square, London W1P 6AE.

CHAPTER 5

DRAMATHERAPY

By Sue Jennings

> *"Drama was in its origins a religious ritual intended to secure the continued life of the community or to avert the consequences of unpurged pollution or the wrath of the dead."*
>
> **Gilbert Murray**

This chapter aims to describe a theoretical and practical framework showing how dramatherapy can be applied in both preventative and curative settings. Dramatherapy practice is based on two working assumptions:-

(i)   there is a close relationship between dramatic expression and healing processes; this is seen in early forms of
theatre and many healing rituals

(ii) through enactment, there is the possibility of insight
learning and change. This process contributes to the
development and maintenance of social and individual
identity (S Jennings, 1981)

However, in order to more fully understand the relevance and importance of these assumptions, it is necessary to look at both the historical context of dramatherapy as well as the contemporary background from which it developed into its current practice.

The Historical Context

As I suggest in my first quotation, the notion of drama having a healing function is not new. Since 'mankind first impersonated another' (S Jennings, 1985), drama has had both a preventative and curative function. Although the very early beginnings are unclear, we can speculate that in the early French cave paintings, where there are examples of humans dressed up as animals, some kind of dramatic ritual was involved. Whether it was to bring good fortune to the hunt, or to stimulate the hunters to a state of readiness, or to celebrate after the hunt, we don't know. The important thing is that it depicts a *change of role* and we can guess it was meant to influence events.

Nearly three thousand years ago in the early Greek theatre, the cults of Osiris and Dionysus among others all had a ritual function. Drama and theatre were not forms of pure entertainment, they were purposeful. There was an intention to the performance and the outcome was to bring about change, or also to influence events. It could be to heighten awareness, it could be to prophesy, or to purge society of anti-social emotions. The latter notion is Aristotle's theory of catharsis whereby the emotions are cleansed by seeing them 'acted out' vicariously. In all these examples, ritual drama was more than entertainment, although it had that function too.

The role of the theatre has shifted in modern times. There is more emphasis now on entertainment for its own sake. Practitioners such as Peter Brook seek to re-vitalise the theatre and make it *immediate*. He suggests that one can reconcile the contradiction of repetition, necessary in rehearsal, if one considers the French word for peformance — 'representation'; it is an occasion when something is re-presented, and therefore is not an imitation or a description of a past event.

"It abolishes that difference between yesterday and today. It takes yesterday's action and makes it live again in every one of its aspects – including its immediacy. In other words a representation is what it claims to be – a making present. We can see how this is the renewal of the life that repetition denies and it applies as much to rehearsals as to the performance." (P Brook, 1972.)

This is a crucial factor in dramatherapy; for example, when someone is re-acting a life event, they are not merely imitating it or describing it in actions, they become it and it brings it into the present in a vital and immediate way.

However it is not just in the historical roots of the western theatre that we can see the origins of healing drama. In many contemporary societies, especially in Asia and Africa, we can witness numerous ritual dramas that have a healing function.

The Temiar tribe of West Malaysia for example have regular seances to maintain a state of well being in the community; they also have specific rituals for curing sick individuals. Experienced shamans call down through song the shy but benevolent spirits who will influence the positive life of the community. Through dance-drama and trance a state of ecstasy is reached which brings about feelings of well being not only for the individual but also for the community as a whole. The seances are like dramatic performance with a particular healing ojective (S Jennings, 1984).

The Contemporary Context

We have seen how in the historical context drama and theatre have always had a healing dimension. This section will deal with the contemporary emergence of dramatherapy practice in Britain where it first became established.

It must be remembered that early arts work in psychiatric hospitals was, for the most part, done by occupational therapists. Certainly in the 1940s and 1950s, painting, music, play reading, amongst other activities were developed in the O.T. department with occasional back-up from visiting performers or the local dramatic society.

Interestingly enough, the move to expand this provision came from outside the hospitals along with the progress being made in the field of drama-in-education. Peter Slade, who initiated 'child drama' which was related to play and developmental psychology, was the first person to put the words drama and therapy together (*Dramatherapy as an Aid to Becoming a*

Person, 1956). Slade was the first 'drama' person to set up a re-habilitation group with psychiatric patients in which they re-hearsed the roles they would have to play once they left the hospital.

During the late 1950s and early 1960s major developments were happening in schools. Drama was becoming a method rather than a product; many schools had regular timetabled drama sessions rather than just an end of term performance, and drama was increasingly seen as an important means of working with less able groups.

In 1962, a group of actors and teachers formed the Remedial Drama Group. Since dramatherapy training, as such, was not yet available members undertook training in analytic group psychotherapy and other forms of psychotherapy. This played a major part in the emerging theoretical basis for practice. The group toured the UK and Europe with special participatory drama programmes for institutions with people who were mentally ill and mentally handicapped. The program-me visited Germany, Holland and Belgium working directly with client groups in movement, mime, and improvisation. Staff were quick to respond and nurses, occupational therapists, psycho-logists and psychiatrists requested staff training programmes to develop the work. It was a difficult transition for staff to join experiential groups. An illustration from a visit to a large teaching hospital in Brussels illustrates the point:-

"The Remedial Drama Group had been invited to work with psychiatric patients in a large teaching institution. The group was about to begin, when in walked a large group of white coated staff with notebooks. The patients stood in a corner with their backs to the wall. The group leader explained that it was a participatory and not an observatory group. There was a moment of fraught silence that seemed like eternity. Then the Senior Consultant removed his tie and joined the group. The rest of the staff followed his example and a staff/patient session evolved, expanded by some more patients who climbed in through the window."

The Remedial Drama Group became frustrated at short-term work and the lack of adequate training provision. The position changed when a base was found in a Baptist church hall, Holloway Road, London, and the group became the

Remedial Drama Centre. The centre worked with clients from the local community, and took referrals from social work agencies. Special groups were run during school hours for school refusers and 'disruptive' groups who were thought to be 'unsuitable' for child guidance. Rehabilitation groups were also provided for psychiatric patients who had been discharged from hospital, and staff training groups for clinicians and teachers were established in the evenings.

The name of the centre reflected its newly emergent focus when it became 'The Dramatherapy Centre'. Although still working with schools and teachers through remedial drama, it had committed itself to the transition to mainstream profession-al health care, especially in psychiatry but also in other areas of disability.

Immediately that transition raised many other issues, such as professionalism, status, relationships with other colleagues and appropriate training, to mention but a few. The past twenty years had seen the resolution of many of these issues.

We can see how Dramatherapy has had several formative influences (see Fig 1 opposite) which include theatre, drama, ritual, drama-in-education and group psychotherapy. Dramather-apy is what its name describes — a meeting of drama and therapy. It is not a collection of techniques, nor is it a means of illustrating a problem. If that were so it would be just a means of copying.

The dramatherapist believes that the experience of the dramatic act in itself is therapeutic, that there is a therapeutic dimension intrinsic to the drama.

I will end this brief introduction to the historical and contemporary contexts with what is possibly the earliest example of dramatherapy in a psychiatric institution. The French psychiatrist Pinel, who contributed radically to reform when he tried to change the prevalent attitudes in the 19th century, was freeing the inmates from their chains in Bicetre and La Salpetriere and decided to use dramatic enactment in role to encourage a client to eat.

The client was ruled by a powerful religious delirium and believed that the only way to escape perpetual damnation was total abstinence. Pinel and the other staff came to his door, acting the part of a judgement here and now, rather than the judgement in the patient's imagination.

"Could the irresistible curse of his sinister idea be counter-balanced other than by the impression of a strong and deep fear?"

One evening the director came to the patient's door,

"with matter likely to produce fear — an angry eye, a thundering tone of voice, a group of the staff armed with strong chains that they shook noisily. They set up some soup beside the madman and gave him precise orders to eat it during the night or else suffer the most cruel treatment. They retired and left the madman in the most distressed state of indecision between the punishment with which he was threatened and the frightening torments of the life to come. After an inner combat of several hours the former prevailed and he decided to take some nourishment." (P Pinel, 1801)

A Simplified Overview Showing the Emergence of Dramatherapy

Dramatherapy evolving in the 20th century from a relationship between therapy and theatre.

 Figure 1

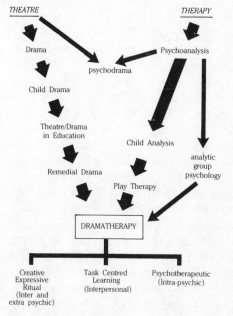

THEATRE

THERAPY

Drama

Psychoanalysis

psychodrama

Child Drama

Theatre/Drama
in Education

Child Analysis

Remedial Drama

analytic
group
psychology

Play Therapy

DRAMATHERAPY

Creative
Expressive
Ritual
(Inter and
extra psychic)

Task Centred
Learning
(Interpersonal)

Psychotherapeutic
(Intra-psychic)

A Theoretical Framework for Dramatherapy

Dramatherapy is based on three main pillars of knowledge: drama and theatre, psychotherapy and social anthropology. It would not be appropriate to develop a detailed theoretical critique at this point, but I wish to outline a theoretical framework for practice. Dramatherapy has contrasting modes of application which need to be understood in relation to a client's overall treatment programme. These modes are not totally discrete but complement each other and may be used developmentally with one group over a period of time. The modes or approaches are:

creative expressive
task centred
psychotherapeutic

The Creative-Expressive Approach

Although we intend that all our drama work is creative and expressive, in this approach to dramatherapy this aspect is emphasised very strongly. The basis is that people can get in touch with healthy areas of themselves (although they may also have problems) and find expression through drama in many different forms. Jungian analyst Rosemary Gordon suggests that part of the creative process is going beyond the usual limits of self, 'self transcendence', and this can bring about new energy, new insights and a heightened experience of self.

What is perhaps the most important is the development of the imagination. This in itself for many people, whether clients or not, can be a very frightening experience. How often have we heard people say, 'I am not creative', 'I have no imagination'? Through the imagination we are letting go of our logic and allowing ourselves to wonder how things were, or how they might be. To be able to imagine needs a reasonably healthy ego, i.e. we need a healthy ego in order to let it go. Much of the work with clients is concerned with developing and building up these strengths through the use of various games and creative structures to get to the point where they can begin to improvise. There is a diverse range of plays that can be used in therapeutic work which often express very eloquently feelings, themes and dynamics.

In creative expressive drama we are developing in the individual the latent capacity to feel confident to take the adventurous leaps necessary to be creative. In this setting the client is both creator and explorer. The focus is on the therapeutic experience of the drama rather than on analysis and interpretation. Voice and body are the media and the imagination is stimulated by the imagination of others.

The dramatherapist needs to feel confident to use a very wide range of dramatic media including movement, mime, masks, scripts, improvisation, games, as well as dramatic stimuli such as props, lighting, sound effects, costume and make up.

This emphasises the central point in this approach to dramatherapy; ie the 'health' approach. Above all, it must be remembered that creative expressive drama is primarily an art form, and although it is being applied therapeutically, it rests firmly within the creative arts rather than being viewed as an 'action' therapy.

The Task-Centred Approach

All of us in our everyday life talk about our roles, meaning the various behaviour we exhibit according to the setting we find ourselves in, and the various sets of expectations we meet.

Many theorists (such as Erving Goffman, 1956) have used the analogy of drama being like life; one can use a dramatic framework to study life and also to change it. Many social scientists have written and worked with role concepts, possibly the earliest was George Herbert Mead in 1934 when he talked of "taking the role of the other".

Currently it is as if the social scientists and dramatists have suddenly become aware of each other, both claiming to know about 'role'; which of course they both do from varying perspectives. A synthesis of their ideas and experience will prove to be a rich contribution to our future understanding.

Many clinicians make use of role-play in their work for life and social skills training, in family therapy and many other situations, without necessarily calling it dramatherapy. However, as I mentioned earlier, dramatherapy is not a series of techniques, and role play is a technique shared by many disciplines.

In this approach to dramatherapy the emphasis is on the learning of readily identifiable skills. It is related to the 'drama of everyday life' ie. how we all are as social human beings. The emphasis is on role repertoire and role flexibility which is why role play is the most common technique used. Games and simulations are also important media.

Task centred work for the dramatherapist will usually be 'corrective' rather than preventative. That is they will be working with groups of clients who need to modify certain aspects of their interpersonal behaviour, or who are lacking in certain aspects of behaviour. Therefore specific programmes will be developed in order to work at changes, modification and new skills.

I must illustrate the paradox of drama in this approach. Even if we are seeking to change the most everyday of roles – such as how to go into a shop and ask for something – what we call a reality situation (reality as contrasted with being a spirit of a mountain in an ancient legend), nevertheless we are using an *imagined* situation to practise it.

If the task was to go into the shop, we would then let all our clients loose in shops but the fact that we are creating an *imaginary* shop in order to practise our role of going into it to ask for something, illustrates how the reality and the non-reality are happening both at the same time. This is the essential paradox in drama. It is at the same time both real and not real.

Thus the dramatherapist can create a healthy working alliance working with the psychologist in transforming the space, the person, the setting into the 'as if'; I am walking into this space *as if* I am going to a shop. This takes us to the actor who does the same thing when he inhabits the role of someone else, to portray it. The client is inhabiting a new role in order to modify it and eventually own it (S Jennings, 1982).

This approach to role play is not asking *why* we have not acquired this or that skill; it is providing the stage for us to enact the means of acquiring it; we are working with *how* in a very task-specific way.

When discussing method I shall look at the various means of establishing this focus and also how to decide which skills need to be developed. "Who is saying I am unskilled and what is going to be done about it? Do I change or does society? Do I have a choice?"

The Psychotherapeutic or Insight Approach

The dramatherapy group represents the scenario for all the individual and collective dramas of the group members with the group scenario representing the scenario of life itself. Dreams and creative expression are seen as ways in which the unconscious can be made manifest. Therefore scenes from past, present and future lives, dreams and fantasies, physical and emotional blocks of different kinds can be worked with in an active dramatherapy session. The crucial point is man's capacity to symbolise, to be able to use representation of thoughts, words and feelings. The focus is on unconscious and latent material that is preventing individuals from healthy emotional functioning. Problems are not just 'acted out' but integrated into the life of the psyche through reflection.

However, the most 'meaningful' work does not necessarily come about from enactment or re-enactment of very specific and defined situations. Very often we are unaware of why we are troubled; if we were aware, we might be less troubled. Therefore it is important in dramatherapy to be able to bring into consciousness material that is unconscious; to make known what is unknown. However this is not necessarily accomplished through verbal communication and analysis. The power of symbolic material lies in the fact that it is symbolic. Frequently an *interpretation* can block the insight being brought into awareness at a *symbolic level.*

Primitive man was very astute when he made sure that his symbolic rituals were enacted at regular intervals throughout the life cycle. However much we try to translate such rituals into the language of the mundane, whatever we decide about their structure and function, there is also something irreducible, that is beyond explanation in our 'ordinary' language.

One of the criticisms of classical psychoanalysis is its reductionism; that the richness of man's symbolic life is reduced to the everyday. The way into the unconscious is through symbols and symbolic re-enactment of a situation. The use of symbols for unconscious projection is staying *with the metaphor,* although bringing it into consciousness.

In this context too I would like to point out how the word ritual has become a perjorative term when used by clinicians. It is often used to describe stereotyped behaviour that to the *observer* appears to have no meaning. What it symbolises is perhaps something that we have not decoded. Whatever our theoretical leaning, whether towards Freud, Jung or others, we are working within a psychodynamic orientation of dramatherapy which means we are working with intra-psychic material. Whichever school of thought we may adhere to, we are discussing an aspect of ourselves that mediates between internal reality and external reality; between the conscious and the unconscious; between repressed material and available material. We are in fact working in the dimensions of the unknown/known and the private/public.

Dramatherapy contrasted with Psychodrama

Perhaps here it would be apposite to distinguish dramatherapy from psychodrama, which originated in America. There is much confusion between the two and people often think they are synonymous. Psychodrama is one particular form and methodology which can come under the *broadest* concept of dramatherapy. Developed by Moreno, a Viennese psychiatrist, in the 1920s and 1930s, it is much more akin to psychoanalysis in that the prime focus is on the *individual* within the group, rather than the group itself. An individual will re-enact current difficulties or past traumas as protagonist with a cast chosen from the group and will seek insight by experiencing the various aspects of the situation of him/herself. Moreno developed his method from the theatre in New York and used techniques from actors' training. Dramatherapy and psychodrama are not sets of techniques; many of their techniques in fact are similar and are shared by other therapies such as Gestalt. They are contrasting and complementary approaches to therapeutic enactment.

The Therapist

The dramatherapist is someone who has had a thorough training in both drama and therapy, has experienced being a client in a dramatherapy group and has supervised practice in relation to clinical application.

You may well ask at this point – so what about the actor or the drama teacher being able to work in creative drama with clients in this way? They after all have the skills, and techniques. I am not denying that the performer and the teacher all have their place in the creative lives of clients, as with all of us. Similarly there are clinicians such as occupational therapists who have the therapeutic training but often lack the developed drama training and experience.

However it does need a trained dramatherapist to safely take an individual or group through the often highly emotional areas, the unchartered territory of dramatic exploration. Drama is a very dynamic medium. Properly harnessed there is no danger, although there is risk. However, ill managed it can prove disastrous not only for the clients but for the facilitator too.

Obviously there are areas of drama work which can be undertaken by other professionals providing they are aware of the dangers. (Advice is always available from the training colleges and the professional association – see Appendix II, pp 223.)

Golden Rules:

(i) Never use ideas and techniques that are unfamiliar to you; you cannot 'do' dramatherapy from a list; if necessary, try them out on colleagues or friends and get feedback on the ideas, your rationale and how they felt about the experience.

(ii) Never use ideas and techniques about which you yourself have no conviction; if you feel certain things are 'silly and childish' then your group will feel the same. You need to *believe* in your methods, otherwise do something else. A good check is to ask yourself, 'How would I feel experiencing this?'

A Practical Framework for Dramatherapy Groupwork

All dramatic media can be useful in therapeutic intervention, and the choice will depend on the goals of the group, the skills of the therapist and the interaction between the group and the therapist. Therefore there are many questions that need answering before the formation and the commencement of the group.

Pre-Group Check List

(i) What is the nature of the group: is it open/closed (ie. does it have a fixed membership or will people come and go)?

(ii) Will the focus be on the learning of skills, or the experiencing of process?

(iii) Will it be based on creative expression/task-centred learning/therapeutic insight?

(iv) What are the aims and goals? How are these negotiated? Where are decisions made? With whom and by whom? How does this relate to the patient's needs and the institutional ethos?

(v) How do you agree your contract with your client group? Is it overt or covert? Is there room for compromise and change? How do your clients know why they come to your group? Do they have a choice?

(vi) What are the ground rules of the group? How are these decided and how are they kept? eg. how do you enforce a 'No Smoking' rule, or regular attendance unless there is serious illness?

(vii) Does your group run for a fixed length of time such as 10 weeks, or a year, or does it carry on without clear endings and beginnings?

(viii) How do you negotiate breaks for statutory holidays? Illness? Annual leave? How do you work at these endings in the material of the group?

(ix) How much of the above is covert and how much is overt and readily available between you and the members of your client group?

The process of the group can be seen under three main headings:

THE BEGINNING: warm-ups and starters;
THE DEVELOPMENT: where it is going;
THE CLOSURE: wind-down and reflection.

I will give examples of material under these three headings and also ideas for the development of a session. These ideas are expanded more fully in *Creative Drama in Groupwork* by S. Jennings, 1986.

The Beginning: Warm-ups and Starters

We often assume, rather like in a recipe book, that we must 'warm-up' our group, yet we rarely ask the following questions which could save us many feelings of anxiety when our groups do not react in the way we expect.

Why am I warming up the group?

What am I warming them up for?

Am I warming up the group for action? Stillness? Concentration? Paired work? Individual work? Small groups? Large groups? Whole groups? Is it a new group, a few weeks old or well established? Are there new members?

What do I do about warming myself up? Both to the group and to the theme?

What do I do about the group that arrives already warmed up? What are the connections between the warm-up and the rest of the session?

Warming up a group is concerned with the group and the therapist developing the energy and focus to approach the task in hand; the warm-up should be linked to what is going to happen next and will often be a stimulus for it.

It will take into account:

● the aims of the group
● the development of the group
● the atmosphere of the group at the start.

To illustrate, it will be very unproductive if a group arrives in a state of anxiety because their routine has been changed if a way is not found in the warm-up of acknowledging the anxiety

204 / THERAPY THROUGH MOVEMENT

and allowing for the transition. However, if the anxiety is the material for the therapeutic group, then do not use a warm-up to dispel it, rather to focus it.

The following are examples of the different ways a group can be started depending on its mood at the beginning. Imagine that a group has arrived in a state of anxiety because their routine has been changed.

(i) If it is a creative expressive group use a warm-up that would allow time for the transition of these feelings into positive working energy; nevertheless, consider improvisational material to do with displacement, sudden change and so on, where the earlier feelings could be expressed within the dramatic media.

(ii) If it is a task-centred group, the feelings can be acknowledged without being explored. A warm-up is needed to dispel the anxiety because it could get in the way of the task in hand.

(iii) If it is a therapeutic group then the feelings would be the very material to examine; so, for example, ask people to move to indicate how they are feeling and to exaggerate that movement and so on. It could be developed through role play.

Let me give an illustration from my own practice of work in a psychiatric hospital. It is winter and I am expecting a group to arrive in the drama room from a back ward.

"The group arrive fragmented and cold from crossing the courtyard to get here; there is a lot of fumbling with coats and woollen gloves, runny noses and a general atmosphere of being 'frozen', both literally, but also metaphorically, because they are so institutionalised.

After greetings and exchanges, I start by getting them to move their different body parts to music, starting slowly and gradually developing the energy. We are using a familiar piece of music that they like. Now we are stretching and doing some breathing exercises finishing the warm-up with 'centering'.

There is a sense of greater freedom and energy, people's bodies are freer and I wonder if this could be a possible theme for the group. I decide to test it by doing an animal game and see who chooses to be what sort of animal. There is a mixture of wild animals, animals in cages and domestic animals. So I decide to develop an improvisation around the theme of 'freedom and restriction' still using the animal metaphor.

I end the group by inviting each group to tell the story of their animals."

This is what is called 'signposting'; pick up a mood or theme in a group, test it and then develop it. Not all moods come as specifically as the one mentioned above, but if we develop the capacity to 'listen' to the group, not just to verbal communication but through our 'antennae', we will sense 'where the group is at'. A caution here: a direct question will often *not* tell you where the group is at; questions such as 'How is everyone?' will usually provoke the response 'All right', or, 'Could be better' . . . a response of social convention!

Warm-ups do not *have* to be physical though on occasion may need to be. If a group arrives already warmed up, it usually means that there is plenty of energy but it is diffuse, all over the place. You will need to bring it into some kind of focus before proceeding with the following activities. It would be unwise to do relaxation exercises to calm the whole group down and then use some energy techniques to warm them all up again; rather than using the energy that was already there!

Warm-ups free the body and the voice for creativity, energise for the task in hand, focus on a particular mood or theme, tune in to where the group is.

The therapist commences *his or her own* warming-up process during the time preceding the group (and possibly the night before). Re-run the scenario of the group in your mind as well as reading through notes so that you are clear at what stage it closed and the potential themes that are around. Make sure you have space before starting the group to shed anything you may have on your mind, and try to free yourself as you enter the group of things that might get in the way. Register in yourself the atmosphere and mood of the group when you enter because it will tell you where the group is, and this may form the basis of the session.

The following are a selection of examples of different warm-ups.

Examples

1. introduce yourself and your favourite food round the group
2. throwing a soft ball, say your name and throw it to someone else

3. say the name of the person you are throwing the ball to

4. think back to when you first woke up this morning and tell the story of what happened until you got to this group (if the group is small then to the whole group, if there are many people, tell it to a partner or small group)

5. hold hands in a circle, close your eyes and be aware of the person on either side of you; how do their hands feel? Would you recognise them by their hands?

6. touch four corners of the room, the ceiling, the floor and six pairs of knees; I will time you, you have one minute. Then re-trace your steps to be back where you started, do you remember whose knees you touched?

7. movement shake out; shake and then stretch different body parts (name them)

8. be aware of your breathing and breathe in and out evenly

9. breathe in and then let the air come out while you make a vowel sound; practise starting the sound small and letting it get louder then softer (higher then lower?).

10. check out that your body does not feel tense, feel 'at home' in your body.

Choose different warm-ups for different situations; several of them can be used specifically with new groups as 'getting to know you' techniques. If they are unfamiliar, try them out with friends and get feedback from them.

The Development

Check that you are not spending so much time warming-up your group that there is little time left for development. No wonder leaders get daunted when suddenly it is ten minutes before the end of the group and they are just getting into depth. It is difficult to be exact in this, but a rough guide will be that the warm-up will take about the first quarter of the time available.

Games

One way of building up confidence and skills in a group is by using different sorts of games structures. This is not the same as using a game as a warm-up, but allows far more developmental time for the games themselves. You and the group will have to choose between:

- familiar and new games
- individual and group games
- competitive and co-operative games
- very active and very still games.

Try to include a variety so that there is contrast. The safety of the game is that it is man made, it has basic rules which are available to everyone and there is some kind of outcome. It has a known structure which makes it secure: a beginning, middle and end.

Games can develop the following: concentration, listening, bodily control, alertness, touching, risk taking, co-operation, self esteem.

EXAMPLES:

Fox and Lambs: one person is fox (it) and uses a cushion to catch someone else by placing the cushion on their chest; lambs can escape being caught by hugging someone else (chest to chest), but only for a count of three.

Doors and Windows: all the group join up to make a large shape with gaps and spaces; people take it in turns to move in and out of every 'door and window', some being very low down, some high up.

Be sure to get the group to contribute their own games, maybe those they can remember from childhood. All books on drama and children's play have a wealth of ideas that can be developed for a games group.

Trust Exercises

Many trust exercises were stimulated by the Encounter Movement and again the literature can act as a resource. Trust exercises can be used to build up trust in a group at the beginning, to explore why people do not feel trusting and also to reassure individuals who may have become distressed.

EXAMPLES:

The Blind Walk: in pairs, one person closes his eyes and the other places a hand on his shoulder and guides him round the room, using no sounds or words. Get yourself into the rhythm of your partner and be aware of any tensions; if you feel they are ready, allow your partner to take some risks. Change over and share the experience.

The Raft: all the group kneel on hands and knees in very close proximity, one or two people (depending on the size of the group) lie on their backs and are gently rocked by the human raft. Later, one person can lie on the back of another, supported by three other people, one for the legs and one each side.

Trust Fall: one person stands in the centre of a circle and the others group closely round; standing straight, the one in the centre 'falls' towards different sides of the group and allows the group members to catch and place him/her upright again.

Sculpts and Spectograms

A sculpt is a visual representation of *what is happening* in an event, or in a situation, or in the here-and-now of a group; it is like taking a photograph of the situation. Sculpts can be directed by one individual or can be a whole group's perception.

EXAMPLES:
Free Sculpt: (often to check out a group that is stuck) define an area in the room to represent the group, and ask everyone to be inside representing how they are feeling at the moment. It will usually contain insiders and outsiders, sub-groupings and power centres; each part of the sculpt can make a statement of why they are there; this will yield material to be developed through role play.

Individual Sculpt: one person has talked about the struggle they are having in their family; suggest they choose members of the group to represent the struggle. (Encourage members to work metaphorically, ie. with the dynamics of the sculpt rather than just literally the people.)

The representation can then be worked with, for example, in movement to resolve the struggle; or a regrouping of how they would like it to be; or after 'doubling' the sculpt (ie. the person speaks on behalf of all the parts of the sculpt so everyone knows who they are), the sculpt can speak to the person and say what they feel; the person can then role reverse with significant parts of the sculpt and speak as they are feeling.

Spectograms belong to the whole family of sculpts and are also known as 'button games' or 'life pictures'. Individuals use objects from around the room, or objects from their pockets or bags, or objects from a special box kept specifically for spectograms (it can contain small objects – buttons, beads, rosettes, buckles, etc). People are asked to make a picture, the title of which is, for example, "My Life Now", or "My Family Now".

They are encouraged not to be too literal and to use the objects to represent not only people, but also ideas, important objects (such as house), feelings, ambitions. The 'picture' can then be shared with a small group or with a partner; give people enough time (say five minutes) to each have a turn; the therapist should remind people of the time very clearly, eg. 'you have one minute to finish telling your partner', and then 'it is time to change to your partner', and so on.

EXAMPLE:

'The Important Things in My Life': use small objects from round the room to make a picture with the title 'The Important Things in My Life'; it can include people, objects, ideas. Share with your partner and say what else you would like to be there.

How you develop the work from the spectogram will depend very much on the type of group you are running; for many groups it is enough to share the spectogram and then to re-arrange it with changes they would like to make if they could; and then to share those changes first with the small group and then with the large group, suggesting possible resolutions.

In some groups the work can then be examined and developed through role play; an issue can be taken from the spectogram and looked at in more depth by setting up a situation, enacting it and role reversing it.

Cautions: sculpts and spectograms should only be used in therapeutic groups where the group is continuous and there is plenty of resource and time for support and follow up. The technique can be very 'instant' and therefore often very disturbing; try it out for yourself and with friends first. Always be judicious when using the spectogram with a person who perceives his life as having nothing in it; the spectogram will just reinforce that belief.

Sculpting can be used outside therapeutic groups for decision making and problem solving. This can be on different scales. I was asked once to go into an institution where the staff morale was very low, so we brought all the staff together as a large group. The use of a sculpt in this setting mobilised some energy for the staff to look at their own dynamics and recognise areas of conflict that needed to be worked on.

Spectograms can also be taught as a skill to help people problem solve; to help when a person cannot make up his mind what to do and there are several choices. By representing the problem visually, it will often become quite apparent what the appropriate decision is.

Spectograms can be used in families for making family decisions; each person in the family makes a spectogram of how they see a particular tricky situation. Thereby everyone sees how the *others* see the situation, which is far more direct than just describing it through words. Solutions can then be worked at through the spectograms.

Role Play

Frequently role play is referred to in the context 'We do role play but we don't do drama', yet most drama work involves some kind of role play. It may be exploratory role play or goal-specific role play, but we are 'in role as another', in enactment and re-enactment ie. in drama.

Role play can be used in various ways to achieve different ends and we need to be clear what sort of role play we are doing and why we are doing it. I will elaborate the two types of role play I have already mentioned – exploratory role play and goal specific role play.

Exploratory role play is open-ended, and enables us to make discoveries about a scene, a character, a situation, ourselves. The essence of exploratory role play is improvisation and this is the core of creative, expressive drama work. It can be approached in several different ways, eg:

EXAMPLE:
Newspaper stimulus: cut out the headlines from various newspapers and let small groups choose one each (perhaps working in groups of four). Discuss the possible story behind the headlines and then dramatise it through improvisation and see what happens.

Or similarly, cut a small piece from a newspaper and use it in the same way. Another variation would be to let all groups have the *same* story and look at their different versions.

Single Sentence Theme: "A man was walking down the railway compartment with a travelling rug wrapped closely round him, it was obvious he was wearing no trousers."

Improvise what had led up to this situation and what happened afterwards.

Many groups will need to do a lot of drama work before they feel ready to improvise. If they do not feel ready you will find that responses are very stereotyped. A skilled dramatherapist can use the stereotypes as a way into deeper level material using careful guidance. However, for disturbed people, staying with stereotypes is a safe way of working and defends against any real engagement. You must consider carefully whether the client is *ready* to improvise, and if not, use a lot of ego-building exercises.

Much of this pre-work can be in movement. The importance of non-verbal work cannot be overemphasised. Very often it can compensate for an important stage in development that has been missed out; for a child may never have learnt about self through play, or this learning may have been very controlled. It is during this period that body image, separation and spatial awareness are all experienced in healthy development. If these stages have not occurred then the adult will have difficulty doing certain forms of drama as well as difficulty in real life roles. Therefore much time may have to be spent on non-verbal work (R Ellis and D Whittington, 1981), games and 'safe' dramatic structures. Again most drama books have examples of all these techniques and several texts have already been mentioned. I will briefly mention some 'safe' structures.

EXAMPLES:

The set scene: On a card, write down several clear scenes with the following:

- the setting (where it takes place)
- the cast (who is in the scene)
- the central theme (what it is about)
- the beginning (how it starts)
- the end (the outcome)

In this type of structure the only improvisation is the middle and this has limited range because the ending is already prescribed.

The set story: Tell an appropriate story for the particular group and then let the group re-enact the story.

Often it is helpful to re-enact other people's stories before enacting one's own life story. Stories of all kinds can be used in creative sessions. (A Gersie, 1984)

The open-ended story: Start off a story in a group and let the group improvise the end; again, the story format will reduce the number of options and allow people to feel safer.

Another way is to say to a group, 'tell a story that must include the following: a cough, two plates and a cat'.

You may want to use play texts as a basis for drama work. Choose small scenes that can be read through and then improvised without the script, or else work with the script but divide it into small units. A good play will include major 'life themes' and participants are often able to make discoveries about themselves through experiencing these universal themes.

However, be on the look out for the client who always wants to play a similar character such as 'the good little girl', or 'the mean old nasty'. Encourage role flexibility in the way you cast the parts, otherwise the 'stock' characters of the play will re-inforce the 'stock' characters of the cast.

Rather than cultivating the idea of 'acting a role', try to establish that we *become* other roles, that we allow a role to inhabit us, otherwise our drama work will not get beyond the 'pretend' stage. However it is a risk to involve ourselves in the persona of another and we need to approach it very carefully.

Goal-specific role play has very clear boundaries. It is role play performed to clearly defined goals. Most social skill work is based on this type of role play; the individuals literally rehearse and practise new or modified life roles. Initially in social skill programmes we may need to break down the role into smaller units such as 'walking into a room', or 'sitting on a chair'. As clients become more proficient, they will be able to simulate scenes from life – either scenes that they find difficult or scenes of which they have no experience.

Simulation is literally a 'slice of life'; it is the reproduction, as near as possible, of a life situation. Simulation is at the core of social skill work because of its specificity. It is hoped that behaviour that has been acquired or modified in social skill work will then generate into other areas of life. There are numerous texts on social skill work (R Ellis and D Whittington, 1981) and I have described the five stages of this form of role play elsewhere (S Jennings, 1982).

We may find that simulation can be useful in other areas. Sometimes we need to simulate the experience before we can begin to explore it, ie. we need to illustrate it to ourselves and the group members, including the therapist. Family and marital therapy can start from a simulation of an actual event that was very difficult, or 'typical'. The scene is reproduced with the main characters and this can be used as a basis for exploration. For example, the main character (the protagonist) could change roles and experience being the other characters. If the scene is one that 'always happens', members of the group can find new ways to end the scene, or even begin it. It can become the material for personal improvisation, and this would usually be in the context of a 'closed' dramatherapy group.

Ending the Group

We mentioned earlier that often people take too long with warm-ups. Often they do not leave enough time for the closure. Whatever type of dramatherapy group you may be running, *at least* a quarter of the time should be spent on the ending. Individuals in the group will take time to *de-role*. It is not enough just to say, 'I am not Mrs Twiggy, I am now Mary Smith'. When people have been involved in this kind of process it takes time to distance themselves from the material and become themselves again, albeit with new insights and experiences.

The most frequent problem with the endings of dramatherapy groups is that people have not had time to properly get out of role, and of course 'wind down'. People need to be able to walk away from the session as themselves and without over dependence on the group. It is not a healthy sign if the group has become so 'groupie' that it has difficulty leaving the room, (often mistaken for nice cosiness); it usually means that too much 'fusion' has taken place and people will need help to individuate again.

I have mentioned here only some of the methods and media that can be used in dramatherapy practice. I have not touched on masks, which are a very vital medium and one with enormous potential for use in therapeutic settings. Material on experiential workshops will provide further ideas. It is hoped that those mentioned will give you some idea of the rich range of material that is available.

Application

Although a large number of people can enjoy and benefit from participation in creative drama, it must not be seen as a universal panacea.

There are groups who can very specifically benefit and there are those for whom it would be contra-indicative. These groups are listed below, and need to be taken as general guidelines. Dramatherapy as a mode of treatment is particularly effective with the following groups of clients:

- isolated and withdrawn children
- maladjusted and disturbed adolescents
- institutionalised withdrawn groups
- geriatric groups, especially those suffering from memory loss (*see Case History I*)
- disturbed families (*see Appendix 3*)
- non-acute psychosis, and other psychiatric disorder other than those listed below (*see Case History II*)
- most groups of mentally handicapped people (*see Case History III*)
- physically disabled groups both with and without additional emotional problems.

It is also very effective with most groups of clients engaged in a programme of rehabilitation, whether from hospital, prison or other settings. Role rehearsal and simulation of the new situation can help the client anticipate the future and acquire some skills to deal with it (*see Case History IV*).

Dramatherapy would not normally be recommended or implemented with the following problems:

- acute psychosis
- extreme hyperactivity
- psychopaths and psychopathic personalities (*see Case History V*)

- post-trauma
- extreme manic depression.

For clients who are totally out of touch with reality, it is usually unhelpful to use 'as if' drama, though movement, dance and body awareness can provide an 'earthing' experience.

When clients are 'flooding' with emotion, for example following bereavement, it is inappropriate to start dramatic enactment. The usual stages of mourning and grief need to be allowed to happen with appropriate support. Drama intervention would only be used when working with *past* history, if, for example, mourning had not taken place.

Case Histories

Application with specific client groups is best illustrated by case history examples; I will also include one that was a contra-indication to dramatherapy.

I: Mona was very aptly named. Every session she sat in a corner and kept up a running commentary of complaints throughout the drama session. She attended a psychiatric day centre. She was usually very bad tempered. She attended the weekly 'open drama group' for all people attending the centre. Verbal drama did not engage her at all.

I designed the next session to be completely non-verbal after the initial greetings. There was total silence in the room so her initial atempt to complain rang out in the room so loud and clear she immediately closed her mouth.

Everyone was slowly moving to music and we were working with elbows, making patterns in the air. Mona began to move her arms and realised she could make her elbows disappear and re-appear again by turning her arm over. She began to work with her arms alternately and then together. Slowly an expression of sheer wonderment came over her face.

Very slowly she was able to develop her body work in very simple patterns; the verbal attacks became modified as her bodily experience expanded.

II: Vanessa was referred to an out-patient dramatherapy group in a psychiatric day centre. She was diagnosed as being overly conscious of cleanliness, had washing rituals and displayed extreme tidiness. She was isolated and withdrawn and rarely mixed socially. When she first attended the group she was polite, pleasant and extraordinarily physically tense. It seemed as if 'she was holding her body together'; simple relaxation exercises were difficult for her and appeared to provoke rather than resolve the tension. The group were given the choice to 'sit or lie' in their most comfortable position, and then we started a story which began with, 'Once upon a time there was a beautiful bird . . .'

Various members of the group began little bits of the story and described the bird's colours, beautiful wings, that it lived in a forest with other animals.

Vanessa's attention to the theme was most marked, and suddenly she broke into a pause and said, "But the bird had been trapped by an ogre, and it could not use its wings, it was quite helpless; the ogre put the bird in a cage and said, 'If you want any food you have to sing for me', but this bird wasn't a singing bird and couldn't do what the ogre wanted; the ogre got very impatient and kept shouting at the bird, 'Sing, can't you, SING'."

(Her voice at this point reached an altogether new pitch with tremendous force, and she accompanied the shouting with violent hand gestures, gesticulating wildly.) I said to her gently, "And then?" There was a long pause and Vanessa said quietly, "Well the bird nearly died because it did not have any food, and the ogre just dumped it in a barn, and it took a long, long time to get better, before it could fly away".

"But it did fly away?" I asked. "Oh, yes", she said with a slight smile, "in the end the bird got strong and was able to fly and was able to live in the friendly forest with all the animals."

Her progress in the group from this session (the fourth) onwards was rapid; she began to work with her own body and to be able to move it without as much tension; it was as if she was having to learn to experience herself all over again. I worked with a lot of movement and voice work and then improvised dance-dramas where she was able to work with many different stories and many different outcomes. Six weeks later she was discharged and keeps in touch occasionally. She went on attending an outside dramatherapy group for twelve months. She had a lot of catching up to do.

III: Bernt is nineteen years old and has spent all his life in a large institution for the severely mentally handicapped. The staff say that his I.Q. is unascertainable in any meaningful way; he may be functioning at a toddler level. The main concern is his repetitive movements which he performs for hours on end in the corner of the ward. He springs backwards and forwards from the ball of one foot to the other; his right arm is held at an extreme angle away from his body, elbow highest, his left hand is brought near his body where he stares fixedly at his first two fingers. (I suggest the reader actually tries this movement out!)

This ritual he can keep up endlessly and any attempt to stop him results in violent reactions, lashing out, and him scampering to another corner to start the movement up again. I started work with him daily on a one-to-one basis and found the spot where he would let me stand without moving away; it was about fourteen feet from him; I started mirroring exactly the movement that he was making. Initially I kept my distance, doing what he did, but always greeting him when I went in and the same when I left. Gradually over the sessions I began to move a little nearer to him, but still keeping up the same movement.

The beginning of the second week he allowed me to stand next to him and he turned his head, there was brief eye contact and he smiled. My next step was to slightly change the movements and to my surprise he followed. (I went side-to-side instead of backwards and forwards.) Then he made a slight change and I followed him. This was a new phase in our relationship as we began to play together, and although the play was very simple, it was a shared activity and carried out without the tensions and compulsion of the initial ritual.

Gradually Bernt was able to join in a small group and share in group activities in movement and play, but whenever he became anxious, he would dash back to the corner and set up the rocking again. However as he gradually became a more regular participant in the group's movement and drama, the need to rock became less and less.

IV: Jennifer had been hospitalised for two years after a psychotic breakdown. Her husband had left her and she was considered ready to live in the community in sheltered accommodation.

Her biggest fear was of not 'being looked after' and it had transpired that she had gone from an overprotective family to an overprotective marriage – that is until her breakdown made it untenable.

It was important in her rehabilitation programme to give some practical reality to the issues of independence and autonomy she had worked on in her therapy. She needed to bring some external validity to the major internal changes she had experienced.

She, with my help, designed a programme of role plays that she said would be difficult for her – including meeting her mother again as an independent single woman. It was important for her to take these initiatives and feel I could help her – rather than me taking over. The way we negotiated and planned served as a model for other interactions she would encounter. When she 'played helpless' it was important for me not to get manipulated into doing it for her.

We ran the series of role plays, one a week for four weeks, leading up to her discharge. It helped her transition not just into the outside world but into 'her new self'.

V: Donald had been referred to the Dramatherapy group by his consultant who said that he was 'very good at acting'; therefore perhaps drama would be helpful to him. I quickly realised what he meant. Donald did not stop acting; a well built man, though not overweight, he was very restless, always moving, and very verbal. His pace was very much faster than everyone else's and he certainly had a lot of skill in 'acting'. He would willingly take on any part going in an improvisation and if others were reluctant, would take on their parts for them; he could switch mood, voice, accent with extraordinary speed, and also had the gift of the entertainer in him which the rest of the group loved. There were times when it became Donald entertaining the group and they would willingly watch and listen.

It was very apparent that Donald's very skill was also his greatest defence; the roles he played did not 'touch' him at all. He could go from extremes of distress or rage without taking a breath. He could not cope with any quiet or stillness and any attempt to introduce a stillness would mean that he would keep up a running commentary throughout it.

Dramatherapy was quite inappropriate for Donald both for himself and also for the rest of the group. He was able to stay quite unmoved by all the experience and manipulate the group into being entertained by him. Also, in a strange way he undermined a lot of their morale because he appeared so dextrous at acting. They felt they could not possibly be as good as he was.

In these case histories as well as in the example of practical material I have endeavoured to bring alive the nature of dramatherapy, a task which is not easy on the printed page. Much work needs to be done in this area. There are still not enough trained people working in hospitals and day centres who can contribute to the work of the multi-professional team. The dramatherapist relates both to the medical as well as the arts practitioners and often mediates between the two.

There is a need for more research to be carried out in dramatherapy. Current research is being developed with the following client groups:

- asthma sufferers
- autistic adults
- deaf adults
- the elderly
- and with a range of handicapped and disabled groups.

There is a lot of unexplored potential in the application of dramatherapy and its potential for change with people who are emotionally disturbed, mentally ill, mentally handicapped and physically handicapped.

Academic research is being carried out in 'Therapeutic Story Telling', 'Myths and the Unconscious', and 'Drama and Healing'.

Summary

In this Chapter I have endeavoured to introduce the reader to the dynamics of dramatherapy, to the historical background and a theoretical framework and working methodology. There are contrasting examples of case histories to illustrate the material as well as examples of specific techniques used. I come back to my earlier statement that dramatherapy is not just a collection of techniques; if it was, then dramatherapists would be no more than technicians.

Dramatherapy is a creative art process which is facilitated within the therapeutic context. All of us know at some level how to do drama because we have played in various ways when we were young. Play is the springboard for the development of drama. However as adults we tend not to play very much at all, so that doing drama, or 'being the other' is seen as childish make believe. Dramatherapy can be dangerous to the client if used without sufficient training and consideration. It is very 'instant' and can produce sudden overwhelming emotion. Properly structured this should not happen, but never try out on clients methods you have not experienced yourself and also tried out on colleagues.

Dramatherapy is both reality and fantasy for our clients, it helps them both to get in touch with themselves as well as to go beyond themselves. It is a total experience because it involves all of us, our bodies, sounds, words, thoughts, feelings, actions . . .

"Repetitive action without symbolic meaning is not dramatic ritual. It is learning by rote like absorbing lists of facts without relating them to meaning. Too often our response to the idea of ritual is that it is unnecessary, primitive, meaningless . . .

Symbolic dramatic ritual can be a medium for socialisation, and can reinforce social identity. Furthermore, it can provide boundaries to periods of change, times of risk, and can provide the security to enable growth in individuals and groups."
(S Jennings, 1979)

Bibliography

Barker, C, *Theatre Games*, Methuen, 1977

Blatner, H, *Acting In*, Spring Pubs., 1975

Brook, P, *The Empty Space*, Penguin, 1972

Courtney, R, *The Dramatic Curriculum*, Heinemann Educational Books, 1980

Ellis, R, and Whittington, D, *A Guide to Social Skill Training*, Croom Helm, 1981

Gersie, A, 'Story-Telling and its Links with the Unconscious' in *Dramatherapy* Vol 7, No 1, 1984

Goffman, E, *The Presentation Of Self in Everyday Life*, Penguin, 1965, 1969

Gordon, R, 'The Creative Process: Self-Expression and Self Transcendence' in *Creative Therapy*, ed S Jennings, Pitman, 1975, re-printed Kemble Press, 1983

Jennings, S, *Remedial Drama*, Pitman 1973, re-printed A & C Black, 1981

Jennings, S, Ed, *Creative Therapy*, Pitman 1975, re-printed Kemble Press, 1983

Jennings, S, 'Ritual and the Learning Process' in *Dramatherapy* Vol 2, No 4, 1979

Jennings, S, 'Dramatherapy: Origins' in *Drama in Therapy*, Vol I & II, eds Courtney, R and Schattner, G, Drama Book Publishers, NY 1981

Jennings, S, 'The Development of Social Identity Through Dramatherapy', paper presented at the 5th International Congress of Psychomotricity, Florence, 1982

Jennings, S, 'Drama, Ritual and Healing', dissertation based on original fieldwork with the Temiar of Malaysia, 1984, London University

Jennings, S, Ed, *Dramatherapy Theory and Practice: A Source Book for Clinicians* 'Dramatherapy: Historical Background', Croom Helm, 1986

Jennings, S, *Creative Drama in Practice*, Winslow Press, 1986 (forthcoming)

Mead, G H, *Mind, Self and Society*, University Chicago Press, 1934

Murray, G, in *Encyclopaedia Britannica*. 'Greek Drama: Origins', 1962 edition, Vol 7

Appendix 1

Training

Recognised long-term training in dramatherapy was established at Hertfordshire College of Art and Design in 1977. Previous to that, most training took place in short intensive courses, summer schools, although there were some ongoing evening groups based in London. Now the British Association for Dramatherapists *(see Appendix 2)* has validated three training courses in this country for awarding dramatherapy qualifications. They are:

Hertfordshire College of Art and Design, 2 year part-time course;

The College of Ripon and York St John, 2 year part-time course;

South Devon Technical College, Torquay, 2 year part-time course.

All these courses operate at a post-professional/postgraduate level and only take students who already have appropriate degrees or certain professional qualifications. All applicants are expected to have drama experience (if not a drama qualification), as well as some clinical experience. It is essential to be 'in post' throughout the course as students are required to run groups in their place of work.

Broadly the syllabus includes: Dramatherapy groupwork, Drama workshops, Dramatherapy theory and clinical theory. There are placements and extensive written assessments. The core of the course is seen as the Dramatherapy group in which students participate for two years working on their own personal development and the dynamics of the group. The course at St Albans has regular supervision of the students' work practice as an integral part of the course. The course is in the Division of Art and Psychology, so that the Dramatherapy students also have contact with Art Therapy students, which makes for a very healthy exchange of ideas and practice.

Dramatherapists are now working in most areas of Great Britain in the NHS, in Social Services Departments, and in the Community. The biggest concentration is in London and the Home Counties and an obvious concentration near the main training courses which will be discussed below.

People interested in Dramatherapy training should write to

the following colleges for information:

Hertfordshire College of Art and Design, Hatfield Road, St Albans (Division of Art and Psychology). The college runs a two-year qualifying course as well as a Summer School and short evening courses.

The College of Ripon and York St John, Lord Mayors Walk, York (David Powley). The College runs a two-year part-time training (intake every two years) as well as various short courses including a Summer School, one-day intensives and evening courses.

South Devon Technical College, Torquay, Devon (Leon Winston). The college runs a two-year part-time course.

Short Courses

Apart from the courses mentioned above, Dramatherapy Consultants runs short courses in Dramatherapy as well as supervision and support groups for practitioners in the field. Courses are held on a regular basis in London and St Albans and intermittently elsewhere. Publications and resource lists are also part of their service. Information from:

Dramatherapy Consultants
6 Nelsons Avenue
St Albans
Herts.

Appendix 2

The British Association for Dramatherapists

The British Association for Dramatherapists is the professional organisation that represents Dramatherapists in Great Britain. Established in 1977, it has regional branches in the North East, North West, Wales, Midlands, Home Counties, and Devon. Full membership is only open to those who have successfully completed a course validated by the Association. Others may join as associate or student members. The Association provides the following for members:

- information, advice and support
- a twice-yearly Journal entitled Dramatherapy
- five Newsletters annually
- links with other professional agencies in the creative therapies and arts
- conferences and seminars
- validation of training courses
- recommendations on professional standards.

The Association is currently negotiating with NALGO (who are representing Dramatherapists) and the DHSS for a salary and career structure for Dramatherapists.

Information from:

Information Secretary
The British Association for Dramatherapists
P.O. Box 98
Kirbymoorside
York YO6 6EX.

Appendix 3

Examples of Family Role Plays based on Case History Material

1 The Clegg Family

Pat Clegg: 28, slim and pretty; always immaculate in herself and her home; used to work as a secretary until she became pregnant. Has decided motherhood was not what she thought it might be, but finds it constantly demanding; she worries about all the mess and the possible dangers to her child.

Michael Clegg: 30, slim, wiry and neat. Plays squash regularly with a colleague from the bank where he works. He is a senior clerk and is ambitious. He adores his wife and did not want children. He accompanies his wife on most outings or else they stay in together. They live in a first floor maisonette, with no garden.

Jason Clegg: 7, slim and dark haired. A very quiet and compliant, obedient child. Answers questions when spoken to, but rarely initiates. As a young child was always given soft toys and balloons to play with. Collects things.

2 The Jones Family

Sarah Jones: 42 and has been at home for many years. Her eldest child has now left home; her second child died quite suddenly at the age of 2 years. Easily aroused and very volatile, she often goads her husband to get him to react; this leads to her screaming at him "Why do you never fight with me?" His very quiet response provokes her even more. The more quiet he is, the more volatile she becomes.

David Jones: 45, a manual worker, who has stayed in the same job all his life and has been married for 20 years. He is small and unprepossessing looking. He is very contained and never expresses his feelings. He always expresses his views calmly and logically, with a judgement approach to life. Sees himself as quite a martyr to his wife's behaviour and is aware the neighbours feel sorry for him when they hear her shouting.

Appendix 4

Useful plays for use in groups (usually short scenes) and for broader therapeutic understanding.

N.B. Be sure to read (if possible see) a play before using it.

Aeschylus THE ORESTEIA (Penguin, the Robert Fagles translation)

Aristophanes LYSISTRATA; THE FROGS

Shakespeare KING LEAR; TWELFTH NIGHT; HAMLET; THE TEMPEST; RICHARD III

Chekhov THE THREE SISTERS; THE CHERRY ORCHARD

Strindberg THE FATHER; A DREAM PLAY

Ibsen HEDDA GABLER

Thomas UNDER MILKWOOD

Jarry UBU
O'Neill LONG DAY'S JOURNEY INTO NIGHT; THE ICEMAN COMETH
Eliot MURDER IN THE CATHEDRAL
Brecht THE MOTHER; MOTHER COURAGE
Miller DEATH OF A SALESMAN; THE PRICE
Williams A STREET-CAR NAMED DESIRE
Osborne LOOK BACK IN ANGER; THE ENTERTAINER
Pinter THE BIRTHDAY PARTY; THE HOMECOMING
Beckett ENDGAME
Albee WHO'S AFRAID OF VIRGINIA WOOLF?
Genet THE MAIDS; THE BALCONY
Wesker ROOTS
Edgar MARY BARNES
Nicols A DAY IN THE DEATH OF JOE EGG; THE NATIONAL HEALTH
Arden HAPPY HAVEN; SERGEANT MUSGRAVE'S DANCE
Orton WHAT THE BUTLER SAW; RUFFIAN ON THE STAIR
Schaffer EQUUS
Ionesco AMEDEE; THE LESSON; THE BALD PRIMA DONNA
Pirandello SIX CHARACTERS IN SEARCH OF AN AUTHOR
Weiss THE MARAT/SADE
The Marowitz version of Shakespeare's "Taming of the Shrew"
Bond SAVED
Gooch FEMALE TRANSPORT
Whitehead ALPHA BETA
Wandor (Ed) PLAYS BY WOMEN (VOL I) (You might find her book "Understudies: Theatre and sexual politics" interesting)
Dario Fo and Franca Rame FEMALE PARTS